World Geography Questionnaires

Asia – Countries and Territories in the Region

Volume IV

Kenneth Ma & Jennifer Fu

Geography Collections

Write to geopublish@gmail.com for more information about this book.

Book Title:	World Geography Questionnaires Asia – Countries and Territories in the Region Volume IV
Author:	Kenneth Ma & Jennifer Fu
ISBN-10:	1453831983
ISBN-13:	978-1453831984

Table of Contents

Introduction 1

Asia 2

Central Asia 3

Eastern Asia 3

Southeastern Asia 3

Southern Asia 3

Western Asia 4

Afghanistan 6

Akrotiri and Dhekelia (United Kingdom) 9

Armenia 10

Azerbaijan 13

Bahrain 16

Bangladesh 18

Bhutan 20

British Indian Ocean Territory (United Kingdom) 23

Brunei 24

Burma 26

Cambodia 29

China 32

Cyprus 40

Gaza Strip (Disputed) 43

Georgia 44

Hong Kong (China) 46

India 48

Indonesia 53

Iran 58

Iraq 61

Israel 64

Japan 67

Jordan 71

Kazakhstan 73

Korea, North 76

Korea, South 79

Kuwait 81

Kyrgyzstan 83

Laos 86

Lebanon 88

Macau (China) 91

Malaysia 93

Maldives 96

Mongolia 98

Nepal 101

Oman 104
Pakistan 107
Philippines 109
Qatar 113
Saudi Arabia 115
Singapore 118
Sri Lanka 120
Syria 122
Taiwan (China) 125
Tajikistan 127
Thailand 130
Timor-Leste 133
Turkey 135
Turkmenistan 138
United Arab Emirates 141
Uzbekistan 143
Vietnam 145
West Bank (Disputed) 150
Yemen 151
Miscellaneous 154
Bibliography 165
Other Books 166
About the Authors 167

Introduction

As a young child, I always enjoyed looking at maps to better understand the world around me. When I heard of the National Geography Bee, I finally got a chance to put it into use. During the contest, I realized how there wasn't just one study guide that covered the entire world effectively. After the contest was over, I thought that the people who had to compete after me shouldn't have to go through the same pain studying from tons of different study guides as well as helping those who simply want to learn more about the world. This got me started on this series of books.

This is the fourth book of the World Geography Questionnaires series, each of which will ask questions on a different region of the world. Each book will be describing important facts about each country in that region in a question and answer format. This book covers countries and territories in Asia – Central Asia, Eastern Asia, Southeastern Asia, Southern Asia, and Western Asia.

As more books are published, a lot of improvements are made based on the feedback. I have decided to do a new edition for the fourth book to restructure some questions, to supplement the country locator images, and to update the content based on new information. If you have any questions or comments, please send an email to geopublish@gmail.com.

This book would have never been possible without the help of my parents, especially my mom, who is also my co-author, my teachers, and my sister. Many thanks to my parents for encouraging me and pushing me to go on, my teacher, Mr. Blair, for starting and widening my interest for geography, and my sister, Hermione, who helped me find the information and get to know it better.

Kenneth Ma

Asia

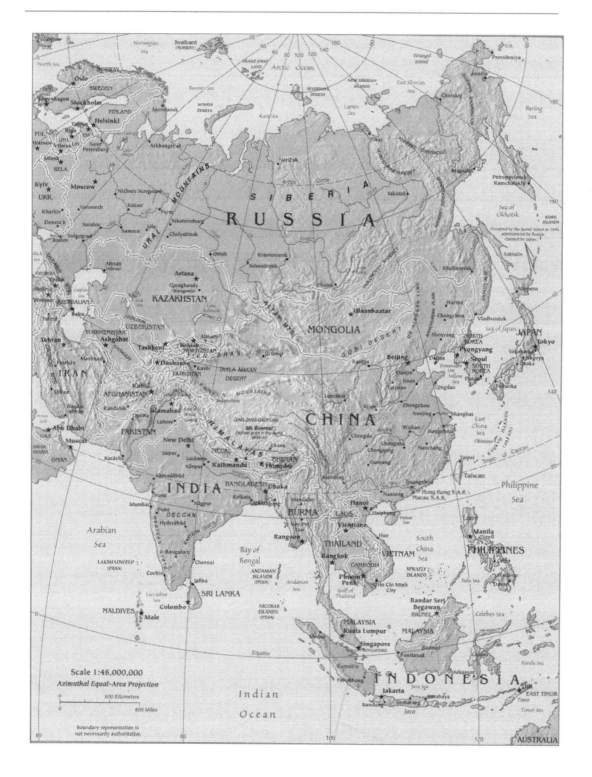

Asia is the world's largest and most populous continent, located primarily in the eastern and northern hemispheres.

The division between Asia and Europe occurs at the Ural Mountains, Ural River, Caspian Sea, Caucasus Mountains, Black Sea, and Turkish Straits (Bosphorus Strait and Dardanelles Strait). Azerbaijan, Georgia, Kazakhstan, Russia, and Turkey are considered part of both Europe and Asia. Although Armenia and Cyprus are entirely in Asia, they are politically European countries. These countries are included in this book, except that Russia is included in the fifth book, Europe.

The division between Asia and Africa occurs at the Suez Canal. Although the Sinai Peninsula is located in Asia, Egypt is considered an African country.

The division between Asia and Oceania occurs between Java and New Guinea. Indonesia spans both areas, but is considered an Asian country. Timor-Leste is also considered an Asian country, due to its being surrounded by Indonesia and once being part of Indonesia.

In Asia, there are 47 countries and a few territories.

Central Asia

Central Asia is a region east of Caspian Sea, west of China, north of Afghanistan, and south of Russia. It is also sometimes known as Middle Asia or Inner Asia. It has historically been closely tied to its nomadic peoples and the Silk Road. As a result it has become a crossroads for the movement of people, goods, and ideas between Europe, West Asia, South Asia, and East Asia. It includes Kazakhstan, Kyrgyzstan, Tajikistan, Turkmenistan, and Uzbekistan.

Eastern Asia

Eastern Asia is a region that covers about 28 percent of the Asian continent. Historically, many societies in East Asia have been part of the Chinese cultural sphere. It includes China, Japan, Mongolia, North Korea, South Korea, and Chinese territories (Hong Kong, Macau, and Taiwan).

Southeastern Asia

Southeastern Asia is a region south of China in the north, east of India, and north of Australia. It lies on the intersection of geological plates, with heavy seismic and volcanic activity. It includes British Indian Ocean Territory (United Kingdom), Brunei, Burma, Cambodia, Indonesia, Laos, Malaysia, Philippines, Singapore, Thailand, Timor-Leste, and Vietnam.

Southern Asia

Southern Asia is a region in the sub-Himalayan countries. It is dominated by the India Plate, which rises above sea level as the Indian subcontinent south of the Himalayas and the Hindu Kush. It includes Afghanistan, Bangladesh, Bhutan, India, Pakistan, Maldives, Nepal, and Sri Lanka.

Western Asia

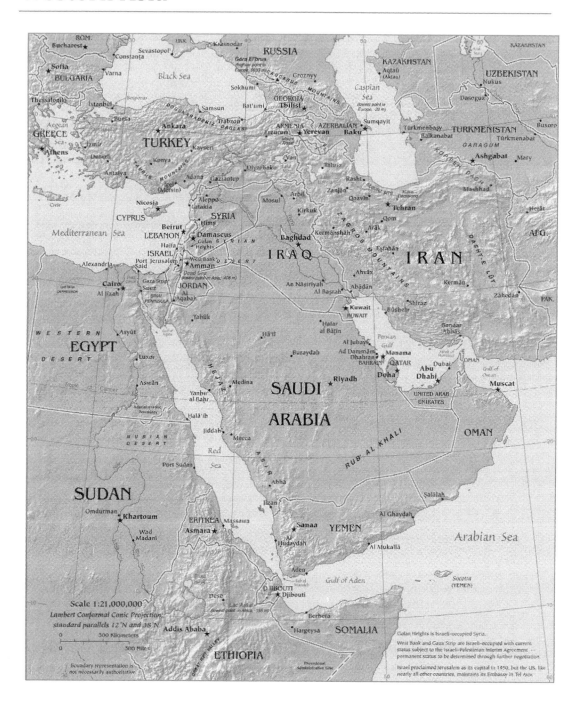

Western Asia is also called the Middle East. It is the historical origin of major religions such as Judaism, Christianity, Islam, and Baha'i Faith. The region generally has an arid and hot climate, with several major rivers (Tigris and Euphrates) providing sources for irrigation water to support agriculture. Many countries located around the Persian Gulf have large quantities of crude oil. It is a strategically, economically, politically, culturally, and religiously sensitive region.

Western Asia includes Akrotiri and Dhekelia (United Kingdom), Armenia, Azerbaijan, Bahrain, Cyprus, Gaza Strip (disputed), Georgia, Iran, Iraq, Israel, Jordan, Kuwait, Lebanon, Oman, Qatar, Saudi Arabia, Syria, Turkey, United Arab Emirates, West Bank (Disputed), and Yemen.

Gaza Strip and West Bank are Israeli-occupied Palestinian territories. Cyprus, Akrotiri and Dhelekia (United Kingdom) politically belong to Europe.

Afghanistan

1. What is the official name of Afghanistan?
   Islamic Republic of Afghanistan
2. Which country borders Afghanistan to the south and east?
   Pakistan
3. Which country borders Afghanistan to the west?
   Iran
4. Which countries border Afghanistan to the north?
   Turkmenistan, Uzbekistan, and Tajikistan
5. Which country borders Afghanistan to the far northeast?
   China
6. What is the national anthem of Afghanistan?
   Milli Surood
7. What is the capital of Afghanistan?
   Kabul (the largest city)
8. What are the official languages of Afghanistan?
   Afghan Persian (also called Dari) and Pashto
9. What type of government does Afghanistan have?
   Islamic republic
10. Which kingdoms established their capitals in Afghanistan?
    Greco-Bactrians, Kushans, Indo-Sassanids, Kabul Shahi, Saffarids, Samanids, Ghaznavids, Ghuris, Kartids, Timurids, Mughals, Hotakis, and Durranis

11. Who unified the Pashtun tribes and founded Afghanistan in 1747?
    Ahmad Shah Durrani
12. Durrani Empire (also called Afghan Empire) was a monarchy centered in Afghanistan and included northeastern Iran, Pakistan, and Punjab region of India. When was it disestablished?
    1826
13. What was the First Anglo-Afghan War during 1839 – 1842?
    It was one of the first major conflicts between Afghanistan and the United Kingdom; it resulted in an Afghan victory, and the United Kingdom withdrew from Afghanistan
14. What was the Second Anglo-Afghan War during 1878 – 1880?
    It was a war between Afghanistan and the United Kingdom/India; it resulted in a British victory and gave the British control over Afghan foreign relations
15. What was the Third Anglo-Afghan War during May 6th, 1919 – August 8th, 1919?
    A war between Afghanistan and the United Kingdom/India; it gave Afghanistan full sovereignty in foreign affairs, but the British managed to reaffirm the Durand Line
16. When did Afghanistan gain independence from the United Kingdom?
    August 19th, 1919
17. When was the Democratic Republic of Afghanistan established?
    April 27th, 1978
18. What was the Saur Revolution?
    A name given to the event that Communist People's Democratic Party of Afghanistan (PDPA) took over the political power to establish Democratic Republic of Afghanistan
19. What type of government did the Afghanistan Democratic Republic of Afghanistan have?
    Socialist Republic, Single-party communist state
20. What was the Afghan Civil War?
    A war started when an insurgency broke out against the People's Democratic Party of Afghanistan in 1978; the war is still ongoing
21. What was the Soviet War in Afghanistan during December 25th, 1979 – February 15th, 1989?
    A conflict involving Soviet Union, supporting the Marxist government of the Democratic Republic of Afghanistan at their own request against the Islamist Mujahideen Resistance (backed by the United States, the United Kingdom, Saudi Arabia, Pakistan, Egypt, China, and Israel); the Soviets were forced to withdraw
22. When was the Democratic Republic of Afghanistan disestablished?
    April 28th, 1992
23. Following the September 11th, 2001 terrorist attacks in New York City and Washington D.C., a United States allied and anti-Taliban Northern Alliance military action toppled the Taliban for sheltering who?
    Osama Bin Laden
24. When did Afghanistan democratically elect the president for the first time?
    December 2004
25. What is the area of Afghanistan?
    251,827 sq mi / 652,230 km^2
26. How long is the coastline of Afghanistan?
    0 mi / 0 km (landlocked)
27. What is the population of Afghanistan?

31,108,077 (by 2013)

28. What is the currency of Afghanistan?

Afghani

29. What is the geographical feature of the terrain of Afghanistan?

Mostly rugged mountains; plains in north and southwest

30. What is the highest point of Afghanistan?

Noshak (24,557 ft / 7,485 m)

31. Noshak is located in which mountain range?

Hindu Kush

32. Hindu Kush divides Afghanistan into which three regions?

Central Highlands (part of the Himalayan Mountains, 2/3 of the country's area), Southwestern Plateau (1/4 of the land), and Northern Plains (Afghanistan's most fertile soil)

33. What is the lowest point of Afghanistan?

Amu Darya (846 ft / 258 m)

34. What are four major rivers in Afghanistan?

Kabul, Amu Darya, Harirud River, and Helmand River

35. What is the longest river of Afghanistan, which rises in the Hindu Kush Mountains?

Helmand River (715 mi / 1,150 km)

36. How long is the Kabul River before it joins the Indus River in Pakistan?

270 mi / 435 km (Afghanistan: 286 mi / 460 km)

37. How long is the Harirud River, located in Afghanistan and Turkmenistan?

684 mi / 1,100 km (Afghanistan: 404 mi / 650 km)

38. What is the largest lake in Afghanistan, located in Afghanistan and Iran?

Hamun Lake (also called Hamoun Oasis, Hamun-e Helmand, 1,500 sq mi / 4,000 km^2)

39. What is the Durand Line?

The border between Afghanistan and Pakistan, which was established after the 1893 Durand Line Agreement between the government of colonial British India and Afghan Amir Abdur Rahman Khan for fixing the limit of their respective spheres of influence

40. What is Afghanistan's first and only national park, announced on April 22nd, 2009?

Band-e-Amir (164 sq mi / 425 km^2), a spectacular region of 6 deep blue lakes separated by natural dams of travertine; it is also a mineral deposit

41. What is the Wakhan Corridor (also called Wakhan Salient and Afghan Panhandle)?

A long and slender land corridor that forms the easternmost extremity of Afghanistan in the Pamir Mountains, connecting Afghanistan to China in the east and separating Tajikistan in the north from Pakistan in the south

42. What are administrative divisions called in Afghanistan?

Provinces

43. How many provinces does Afghanistan have?

48

44. What is the climate of Afghanistan?

Arid to semiarid; cold winters and hot summers

45. What are the natural resources of Afghanistan?

Natural gas, petroleum, coal, copper, chromite, talc, barites, sulfur, lead, zinc, iron ore, salt, and precious and semiprecious stones

46. What are the natural hazards of Afghanistan?

Damaging earthquakes occur in Hindu Kush mountains; flooding; droughts
47. What are the religions of Afghanistan?
Sunni Muslim 80%, Shia Muslim 19%, other 1%
48. What are the ethnic groups of Afghanistan?
Pashtun 42%, Tajik 27%, Hazara 9%, Uzbek 9%, Aimak 4%, Turkmen 3%, Baloch 2%, other 4%

Akrotiri and Dhekelia (United Kingdom)

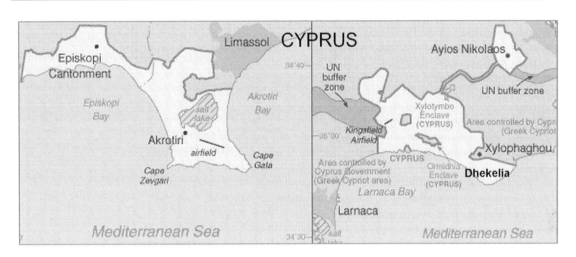

49. What are Akrotiri and Dhekelia?
British overseas territories
50. Akrotiri and Dhekelia are located on the coast of which country?
Cyprus
51. What is the administrative centre of Akrotiri and Dhekelia?
Episkopi
52. What are the official languages of Akrotiri and Dhekelia?
English and Greek
53. The Akrotiri and Dhekelia Sovereign Base Areas were created in 1960 by which agreement, when Cyprus achieved independence from the United Kingdom?
Zurich and London Agreement

54. What is the area of Akrotiri?
    47 sq mi / 123 km^2
55. What is the area of Dhekelia?
    50 sq mi / 131 km^2
56. How long is the coastline of Akrotiri?
    35 mi / 56 km
57. How long is the coastline of Dhekelia?
    17 mi / 27 km
58. What is the population of Akrotiri and Dhekelia?
    15,700 (by 2013)

Armenia

59. What is the official name of Armenia?
    Republic of Armenia
60. Which country borders Armenia to the west and southwest?
    Turkey
61. Which country borders Armenia to the north?
    Georgia
62. Which country borders Armenia to the east and has an exclave, named Nakhchivan, that borders Armenia to the south?
    Azerbaijan
63. Which country borders Armenia to the south?
    Iran

64. What is the motto of Armenia?
    One Nation, One Culture
65. What is the national anthem of Armenia?
    Our Fatherland
66. What is the capital of Armenia?
    Yerevan (the largest city)
67. What is the official language of Armenia?
    Armenian
68. What type of government does Armenia have?
    Presidential republic
69. When did Armenia become the first nation to adopt Christianity as a state religion?
    301
70. Despite periods of autonomy, over the centuries Armenia came under the sway of which empires?
    Roman, Byzantine, Arab, Persian, Russian, and Ottoman
71. What was the Armenian Genocide (also called Armenian Holocaust, Armenian Massacres and Great Crime)?
    The deliberate and systematic destruction of about 1 million Armenians of Ottoman Empire during 1915 – 1918
72. Eastern Armenia was ceded by the Ottomans to which country in 1828?
    Russia
73. What was the Democratic Republic of Armenia (also known called the First Republic of Armenia)?
    It was the first modern establishment of an Armenian republic, established in the former territory of Eastern Armenia
74. When did the Democratic Republic of Armenia exist?
    May 26th, 1918 – December 2nd, 1920
75. What was the Turkish-Armenian War during September 24th, 1920 – December 2nd, 1920?
    A conflict fought between the Democratic Republic of Armenia and the Turkish Revolutionaries; Armenia was forced to give up over half of its territory
76. Armenia was conquered by which country in 1920?
    Soviet Union
77. In 1921, the Soviet Union and Turkey signed the Treaty of Kars, in which Turkey ceded Adjara to the Soviet Union in exchange for the Kars territory. The Kars territory included which part of Armenia?
    The ancient city of Ani and Mount Ararat
78. Mount Ararat (16,854 ft / 5,137 m), the highest point of Lesser Caucasus Mountains, is located in Turkey. Why is it important to Armenia?
    Because it was historically part of Armenia, it is clearly visible in Armenia, and it is regarded by the Armenians as a symbol of their land
79. When was the Armenian Soviet Socialist Republic (also called the Second Republic of Armenia) established?
    December 30th, 1922
80. The Soviet Union assigned which region that was primarily Armenian-populated to the Soviet Azerbaijan in the 1920s?

Nagorno-Karabakh

81. When did Armenia gain independence from the Soviet Union?
    September 21st, 1991
82. Who was the legendary founder of Armenia?
    Haik, a chieftain who called on his kinsmen to unite into a single nation, thus forming Armenia
83. What is the area of Armenia?
    11,484 sq mi / 29,743 km^2
84. How long is the coastline of Armenia?
    0 mi / 0 km (landlocked)
85. What is the population of Armenia?
    2,974,184 (by 2013)
86. What is the currency of Armenia?
    Dram
87. What is the geographical feature of the terrain of Armenia?
    Armenian Highland with mountains; little forest land; fast flowing rivers; good soil in Aras River valley
88. What is the highest point of Armenia?
    Aragats Lerrnagagat' (13,419 ft / 4,090 m)
89. Aragats Lerrnagagat' is located in which mountain range?
    Lesser Caucasus Mountains
90. What is the lowest point of Armenia?
    Debed River (1,312 ft / 400 m)
91. Armenia was called Nairi. What does Nairi mean?
    Land of the lakes and rivers
92. What is the longest river of Armenia, which forms part of the geographic border between Armenia and Turkey?
    Akhurian River (116 mi / 186 km)
93. What is the second longest river of Armenia, located in Turkey, Armenia, Iran, and Azerbaijan?
    Araks River (665 mi / 1,072 km, Armenia: 98 mi / 158 km)
94. What is the third longest river of Armenia, located in Armenia and Azerbaijan?
    Vorotan River (111 mi / 178 km, Armenia: 74 mi / 119 km)
95. The Akhurian River and Vorotan River are tributaries of which river?
    Araks River
96. What is the largest lake in Armenia?
    Lake Sevan (363 sq mi / 940 km^2)
97. What is the surface elevation of Lake Sevan?
    6,230 ft / 1,899 m
98. How many rivers and streams flow into Lake Sevan?
    28
99. Lake Sevan and which two lakes were three great lakes of the historical Armenian Kingdom, collectively referred to as the Seas of Armenia?
    Lake Van (Turkey) and Lake Urmia (Iran)
100. Which national parks are located in Armenia?

Dilijan National Park and Sevan National Park

101. What are administrative divisions called in Armenia?
Provinces

102. How many provinces does Armenia have?
11

103. What is the climate of Armenia?
Highland continental, hot summers, cold winters

104. What are the natural resources of Armenia?
Small deposits of gold, copper, molybdenum, zinc, and bauxite

105. What are the natural hazards of Armenia?
Occasionally severe earthquakes; droughts

106. What are the religions of Armenia?
Armenian Apostolic 94.7%, other Christian 4%, Yezidi (monotheist with elements of nature worship) 1.3%

107. What are the ethnic groups of Armenia?
Armenian 97.9%, Yezidi (Kurd) 1.3%, Russian 0.5%, other 0.3%

Azerbaijan

108. What is the official name of Azerbaijan?
Republic of Azerbaijan

109. Which country borders Azerbaijan to the northwest?
Georgia

110. Which country borders Azerbaijan to the west?

13

Armenia
111. Which country borders Azerbaijan to the south?
Iran
112. Which country borders Azerbaijan to the north?
Russia
113. Which body of water lies to the east of Azerbaijan?
Caspian Sea
114. Azerbaijan has an exclave. What is its name?
Nakhichevan
115. Nakhichevan is separated from Azerbaijan by which country?
Armenia
116. What is the national anthem of Azerbaijan?
March of Azerbaijan
117. What is the capital of Azerbaijan?
Baku (the largest city)
118. What is the official language of Azerbaijan?
Azerbaijani
119. What type of government does Azerbaijan have?
Presidential Republic
120. Over the years, Azerbaijan has been occupied by which empires?
Ottoman Empire, Persia, the United Kingdom and Russia
121. What was the People's Republic of Azerbaijan (also called the Azerbaijan Democratic Republic) during May 28th, 1918 – April 27th, 1920?
It was the first successful attempt to establish a modern parliamentary republic in the Muslim world at the present-day Azerbaijan
122. What was the capital of People's Republic of Azerbaijan before it changed to Baku in September 1918?
Ganja
123. What was the Armenian-Azerbaijani War?
A series of brutal conflicts between Armenia and Azerbaijan in 1918 – 1920; it resulted in an Azerbaijanian victory and the Karabakh territory became a part of Azerbaijan
124. What were the March Days (also called March Events) during March 30th, 1918 – April 2nd, 1918?
An inter-ethnic warfare during the Russian Civil War, which resulted in 3000 to 12,000 Azerbaijanis and other Muslims in Baku massacred by Armenian Revolutionary Federation and Bolshevik forces
125. What was the Battle of Baku during August 26th, 1918 – September 14th, 1918?
A warfare between coalitions of the Ottoman-Azerbaijani forces and the Bolshevik-Armenian Revolutionary Federation-Baku Soviet forces, later succeeded by the British-Armenian-White Russian forces
126. What were the September Days during September 1918?
The retaliation for the March Days during the Russian Civil War, which resulted in 10,000 to 20,000 ethnic Armenians massacred by the Ottoman Army of Islam supported by local Azerbaijanis when they captured Baku
127. What was the Shusha Pogrom of 1920 (also called Massacre of Shusha)?

It was a violent riot directed against the ethnic Armenian population of Shusha, in Nagorno-Karabagh, during March 22nd – March 26th, 1920, which resulted 20,000 – 30,000 Armenian death

128. When was the Azerbaijan Soviet Socialist Republic established?
April 28th, 1920

129. When did Azerbaijan gain independence from the Soviet Union?
August 30th, 1991

130. What was the Nagorno-Karabakh War during February 1988 – May 1994?
It was an armed conflict over Nagorno-Karabakh between Nagorno-Karabakh backed Armenia, and the Republic of Azerbaijan; it resulted in an Armenian victory, and Nagorno-Karabakh became a de facto independent republic, though it is still a de jure part of Azerbaijan

131. What is the area of Azerbaijan?
33,436 sq mi / 86,600 km^2

132. How long is the coastline of Azerbaijan?
0 mi / 0 km (landlocked)

133. How long does Azerbaijan border Caspian Sea?
443 mi / 713 km

134. What is the population of Azerbaijan?
9,590,159 (by 2013)

135. What is the currency of Azerbaijan?
Manat

136. What is the geographical feature of the terrain of Azerbaijan?
Large, flat Kur-Araz Ovaligi (also called Kura-Araks Lowland, much of it below sea level) with Great Caucasus Mountains to the north, Qarabag Yaylasi (also called Karabakh Upland) in west; Baku lies on Abseron Yasaqligi (also called Apsheron Peninsula) that juts into Caspian Sea

137. What is the highest point of Azerbaijan?
Bazarduzu Dagi (14,715 ft / 4,485 m)

138. What is the lowest point of Azerbaijan?
Caspian Sea (92 ft / -28 m)

139. Why do many of Azerbaijan islands in Caspian Sea hold significant geopolitical and economic importance?
Oil reserves

140. How many rivers are there in Azerbaijan?
8,359

141. How many rivers are longer than 62 mi (100 km) in Azerbaijan?
24

142. What are major rivers in Azerbaijan?
Agstafa, Araz, Ganikh, Kura, Pirsaat, Qabirri, Turyan, and Vilesh

143. What is the longest river in Azerbaijan, located in Turkey, Georgia, and Azerbaijan?
Kura River (941 mi / 1,515 km, Azerbaijan: 563 mi / 906 km)

144. What is the largest artificial lake in Azerbaijan?
Mingäcevir Reservoir (234 sq mi / 605 km^2)

145. What is the largest natural lake in Azerbaijan?

Lake Hajikabul (6 sq mi / 16 km^2)

146. What are national parks in Azerbajian?
Absheron National Park, Ag-Gol National Park, Altyaghach National Park, Hirkan National Park, Ordubad National Park, Shirvan National Park, and Shakhdag National Park

147. Which national park, located in northern Azerbaijan, is the largest national park in the whole Caucasus mountain range?
Shakhdag National Park (447 sq mi / 1,159 km^2)

148. What are administrative divisions called in Azerbaijan?
Rayons

149. How many rayons does Azerbaijan have?
59 (plus 11 cities, 1 autonomous republic)

150. What is the climate of Azerbaijan?
Dry, semiarid steppe

151. What are the natural resources of Azerbaijan?
Petroleum, natural gas, iron ore, nonferrous metals, and bauxite

152. What are the natural hazards of Azerbaijan?
Droughts

153. What are the religions of Azerbaijan?
Muslim 93.4%, Russian Orthodox 2.5%, Armenian Orthodox 2.3%, other 1.8%

154. What are the ethnic groups of Azerbaijan?
Azeri 90.6%, Dagestani 2.2%, Russian 1.8%, Armenian 1.5%, other 3.9%

Bahrain

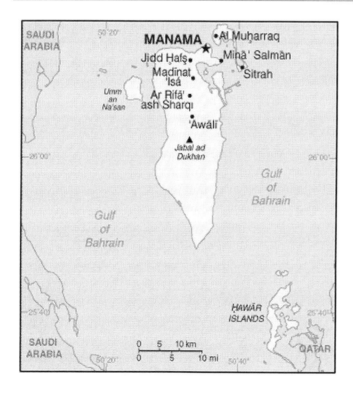

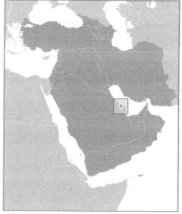

155. What is the official name of Bahrain?
Kingdom of Bahrain

156. Bahrain is an archipelago of how many islands?
32

157. Bahrain is surrounded by which shallow inlet of Persian Gulf?
Gulf of Bahrain

158. Qatar is at which direction of Bahrain?
Southeast

159. Saudi Arabia is at which direction of Bahrain?
West

160. Saudi Arabia is connected to Bahrain via which causeway?
King Fahd Causeway (17 mi / 28 km)

161. Which causeway is planned between Qatar and Bahrain?
Qatar-Bahrain Friendship Causeway (25 mi / 40 km)

162. What is the national anthem of Bahrain?
Our Bahrain

163. What is the capital of Bahrain?
Manama (the largest city)

164. What is the official language of Bahrain?
Arabic

165. What type of government does Bahrain have?
Constitutional monarchy

166. Over the years, Bahrain has come under the influence of which empires?
Sumerian, Assyrian, Babylonian, Persian, Portuguese, and Arab

167. In which year did Bahrain gain independence from Persia?
1783

168. When did Bahrain become a British protectorate?
December 2nd, 1880

169. When did Bahrain gain independence from the United Kingdom?
August 15th, 1971

170. What is the area of Bahrain?
286 sq mi / 741 km^2

171. How long is the coastline of Bahrain?
100 mi / 161 km

172. What is the population of Bahrain?
1,281,332 (by 2013)

173. What is the currency of Bahrain?
Bahraini Dinar

174. What is the geographical feature of the terrain of Bahrain?
Mostly low desert plain rising gently to low central escarpment

175. What is the highest point of Bahrain?
Jabal ad Dukhan (400 ft / 122 m)

176. What is the lowest point of Bahrain?
Persian Gulf (0 ft / 0 m)

177. Which island did Bahrain return to Qatar on March 2001?

Jenan

178. What is the largest island in Bahrain?
Bahrain Island (221 sq mi / 572 km^2)

179. What are administrative divisions called in Bahrain?
Governorates

180. How many governorates does Bahrain have?
5

181. What is the climate of Bahrain?
Periodic droughts; dust storms

182. What are the natural resources of Bahrain?
Oil, associated and nonassociated natural gas, fish, and pearls

183. What are the natural hazards of Bahrain?
Arid; mild, pleasant winters; very hot, humid summers

184. What are the religions of Bahrain?
Muslim (Shia and Sunni) 81.2%, Christian 9%, other 9.8%

185. What are the ethnic groups of Bahrain?
Bahraini 62.4% and non-Bahraini 37.6%

Bangladesh

186. What is the official name of Bangladesh?
People's Republic of Bangladesh

187. Which country borders Bangladesh to the west, north, and east?
India

188. Which country borders Bangladesh to the southeast?
    Burma
189. Which body of water lies to the south of Bangladesh?
    Bay of Bengal
190. What is the national anthem of Bangladesh?
    My Golden Bangla
191. What is the capital of Bangladesh?
    Dhaka (the largest city)
192. What is the official language of Bangladesh?
    Bangla
193. What type of government does Bangladesh have?
    Parliamentary Republic
194. What is Bengal?
    A historical and geographical region in the present-day Bangladesh and the Indian state of West Bengal
195. When did Bangladesh become part of British India?
    May 26th, 1770
196. Bengal province of British India divided on August 15th, 1947. The eastern part becomes East Bengal province of which country?
    Pakistan
197. When was East Bengal renamed as East Pakistan?
    October 14th, 1955
198. When did East Pakistan (as Bangladesh) gain independence from West Pakistan?
    March 26th, 1971
199. What was the Bangladesh Liberation War during March 26th, 1971 – December 16th, 1971?
    It was an armed conflict pitting East Pakistan and India against West Pakistan; East Pakistan was victorious and Bangladesh was granted independence
200. What is the area of Bangladesh?
    55,583 sq mi / 143,998 km^2
201. How long is the coastline of Bangladesh?
    360 mi / 580 km
202. What is the population of Bangladesh?
    163,654,860 (by 2013)
203. What is the currency of Bangladesh?
    Taka
204. What is the geographical feature of the terrain of Bangladesh?
    Mostly flat alluvial plain; hilly in southeast
205. What is the highest point of Bangladesh?
    Keokradong (4,035 ft / 1,230 m)
206. What is the lowest point of Bangladesh?
    Indian Ocean (0 ft / 0 m)
207. About how many rivers are there in Bangladesh?
    800
208. The Ganges Delta, consisting of Bangladesh and West Bengal, is formed at the confluence of which rivers and their tributaries?

Ganges River (also called Padma), Brahmaputra River (also called Jamuna), and the Surma-Meghna River System

209. How long is the Surma-Meghna River System, located in India and Bangladesh?
588 mi / 946 km, Bangladesh: 416 mi / 669 km)

210. What are natural lakes in Bangladesh?
Bagakain Lake, Dhanmondi Lake, and Madhobpur Lake

211. What are artificial lakes in Bangladesh?
Foy's Lake and Kaptai Lake

212. Which beach in Bangladesh is the world's longest natural sandy sea beach?
Cox's Bazar Beach (78 mi / 125 km)

213. Which national parks are located in Bangladesh?
Bhawal National Park, Himchari National Park, Kaptai National Park, Khadimnagar National Park, Lawachara National Park, Medha Kassapia National Park, Modhupur National Park, Nijhum Dweep National Park, Satchari National Park, and Ramsagar National Park

214. What is the largest national park in Bangladesh, located on the island of Nijhum Dweep?
Nijhum Dweep National Park (63 sq mi / 164 km^2)

215. How many exclaves of Bangladeshi are within India?
92

216. What are administrative divisions called in Bangladesh?
Divisions

217. How many divisions does Bangladesh have?
7

218. What is the climate of Bangladesh?
Tropical; mild winter (October to March); hot, humid summer (March to June); humid, warm rainy monsoon (June to October)

219. What are the natural resources of Bangladesh?
Natural gas, arable land, timber, and coal

220. What are the natural hazards of Bangladesh?
Droughts; cyclones; much of the country routinely inundated during the summer monsoon season

221. What are the religions of Bangladesh?
Muslim 83%, Hindu 16%, other 1%

222. What are the ethnic groups of Bangladesh?
Bengali 98%, other 2% (includes tribal groups, non-Bengali Muslims)

Bhutan

223. What is the official name of Bhutan?
Kingdom of Bhutan

224. Which country borders Bhutan to the west, east, and south?
India

225. Which country borders Bhutan to the north?
China

226. What is the national anthem of Bhutan?
The Thunder Dragon Kingdom

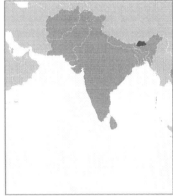

227. What is the capital of Bhutan?
Thimphu (the largest city)

228. What is the official language of Bhutan?
Dzongkha

229. What type of government does Bhutan have?
Constitutional Monarchy

230. The United Kingdom and Bhutan signed which treaty on November 11th, 1865, under which Bhutan ceded territories in Assam Duars, Bengal Duars, and Dewangiri to India, in return for an annual subsidy of 50,000 rupees?
Treaty of Sinchulu

231. The United Kingdom and Bhutan signed which treaty on January 8th, 1910, under which British agreed not to interfere in Bhutanese internal affairs and Bhutan allowed the United Kingdom to direct its foreign affairs?
Treaty of Punakha

232. India and Bhutan signed which treaty on August 8th, 1949, under which India agreed not to interfere in Bhutan's internal affairs, agreed to increase the annual subsidy to 500,000 rupees per year, and also returned Dewangiri?
Treaty of Peace and Friendship

233. India and Bhutan signed which treaty on February 8th, 2007, under which India allowed Bhutan greater autonomy in conducting its foreign policy?
Indo-Bhutan Friendship Treaty

234. When did Bhutan become a democracy?
July 18th, 2008

235. What is the area of Bhutan?
14,824 sq mi / 38,394 km^2

236. How long is the coastline of Bhutan?
    0 mi / 0 km (landlocked)
237. What is the population of Bhutan?
    725,296 (by 2013)
238. What is the currency of Bhutan?
    Ngultrum
239. What is the geographical feature of the terrain of Bhutan?
    Mostly mountainous with some fertile valleys and savanna
240. What is the highest point of Bhutan?
    Kula Kangri (24,780 ft / 7,553 m)
241. Kula Kangri is located in which mountain range?
    Himalaya Range
242. What is the lowest point of Bhutan?
    Drangme Chhu (318 ft / 97 m)
243. What are major rivers in Bhutan?
    Manas River, Amo Chu (also called Torsa), Wong Chu (also called Raidak), and Mo Chu (also called Sankosh)
244. What is the longest river in Bhutan?
    Manas River (234 mi / 376 km, Bhutan: 169 mi / 272 km)
245. About how many glacial lakes are there in Bhutan?
    More than 2,600
246. What is the largest glacial lake in Bhutan?
    Lake Thorthormi (1.3 sq mi / 3.4 km^2)
247. What are national parks in Bhutan?
    Jigme Dorji National Park, Jigme Singye Wangchuck National Park, Royal Manas National Park, and Thrumshingla National Park
248. What is the largest national park in Bhutan, located in the northwestern part of Bhutan, which is home to many wild animals and a wide variety of Himalayan herbs?
    Jigme Dorji National Park (1,679 sq mi / 4,350 km^2)
249. What are administrative divisions called in Bhutan?
    Districts
250. How many districts does Bhutan have?
    20
251. What is the climate of Bhutan?
    Varies; tropical in southern plains; cool winters and hot summers in central valleys; severe winters and cool summers in Himalayas
252. What are the natural resources of Bhutan?
    Timber, hydropower, gypsum, and calcium carbonate
253. What are the natural hazards of Bhutan?
    Violent storms from the Himalayas; frequent landslides during the rainy season
254. What are the religions of Bhutan?
    Lamaistic Buddhist 75%, Indian- and Nepalese-influenced Hinduism 25%
255. What are the ethnic groups of Bhutan?
    Bhote 50%, ethnic Nepalese 35% (includes Lhotsampas - one of several Nepalese ethnic groups), indigenous or migrant tribes 15%

British Indian Ocean Territory (United Kingdom)

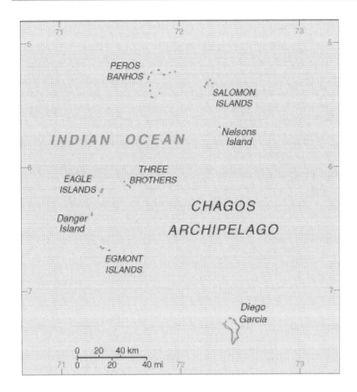 

256. What is the British Indian Ocean Territory?
     An overseas territory of the United Kingdom
257. The British Indian Ocean Territory is surrounded by which body of water?
     Indian Ocean
258. What is the largest island in the British Indian Ocean Territory, located in the Chagos Archipelago (also called Oil Islands)?
     Diego Garcia (10 sq mi / 27 km²)
259. Diego Garcia is the site of a joint military facility for the United Kingdom and which country?
     United States
260. What is the motto of British Indian Ocean Territory?
     Limuria is in our charge
261. What is the capital of British Indian Ocean Territory?
     Diego Garcia (the largest city)
262. What is the official language of British Indian Ocean Territory?
     English
263. When was British Indian Ocean Territory established from parts of Seychelles and Mauritius?
     November 8th, 1965

264. When were Aldabra, Farquhar and Desroches returned to Seychelles?
June 23rd, 1976

265. What is the area of British Indian Ocean Territory?
20,998 sq mi / 54,400 km^2

266. How long is the coastline of British Indian Ocean Territory?
434 mi / 698 km

267. What is the permanent population of British Indian Ocean Territory?
0

268. What is the currency of British Indian Ocean Territory?
US Dollar

269. What is the geographical feature of the terrain of British Indian Ocean Territory?
Flat and low (most areas do not exceed two meters in elevation)

270. What is the highest point of British Indian Ocean Territory?
Unnamed location on Diego Garcia (49 ft / 15 m)

271. What is the lowest point of British Indian Ocean Territory?
Indian Ocean (0 ft / 0 m)

272. What is the climate of British Indian Ocean Territory?
Tropical marine; hot, humid, moderated by trade winds

273. What are the natural resources of British Indian Ocean Territory?
Coconuts, fish, and sugarcane

Brunei

274. What is the official name of Brunei?
State of Brunei Darussalam

275. Which body of water lies to the west of Brunei?
South China Sea
276. Which country borders Brunei to the west, south, and east?
Malaysia
277. Which division in Malaysia separate Brunei into two parts?
Limbang
278. Brunei is located on which island?
Borneo
279. What is the motto of Brunei?
Always in service with God's guidance
280. What is the national anthem of Brunei?
God Bless the Sultan
281. What is the capital of Brunei?
Bandar Seri Begawan (the largest city)
282. What is the official language of Brunei?
Malay
283. What type of government does Brunei have?
Constitutional sultanate
284. In which year was Brunei founded?
1363
285. What was the Castille War?
A war in which Spain invaded the capital of Brunei on April 16th, 1578 and annexed Brunei on April 20th, 1578
286. When did Spanish rule of Brunei end?
June 26th, 1578
287. In which year was the name State of Brunei Darussalam adopted?
1425
288. When did Brunei become a British protectorate?
September 17th, 1888
289. When did Brunei gain independence from the United Kingdom?
January 1st, 1984
290. What is the area of Brunei?
2,225 sq mi / 5,765 km^2
291. How long is the coastline of Brunei?
100 mi / 161 km
292. What is the population of Brunei?
415,717 (by 2013)
293. What is the currency of Brunei?
Brunei Dollar
294. What is the geographical feature of the terrain of Brunei?
Flat coastal plain rises to mountains in east; hilly lowland in west
295. What is the highest point of Brunei?
Bukit Pagon (6,070 ft / 1,850 m)
296. What is the lowest point of Brunei?
South China Sea (0 ft / 0 m)

297. What are major rivers in Brunei?
Brunei River and Pandaruan River
298. What is the largest lake in Brunei?
Merimbun Lake
299. How large is Ulu Temburong National Park, which protects a large area of virgin Temburong forests in Brunei?
193 sq mi / 500 km^2
300. What are administrative divisions called in Brunei?
Districts
301. How many districts does Brunei have?
4
302. What is the climate of Brunei?
Tropical; hot, humid, rainy
303. What are the natural resources of Brunei?
Petroleum, natural gas, and timber
304. What are the natural hazards of Brunei?
Typhoons, earthquakes, and severe flooding are rare
305. What are the religions of Brunei?
Muslim (official) 67%, Buddhist 13%, Christian 10%, other (includes indigenous beliefs) 10%
306. What are the ethnic groups of Brunei?
Malay 66.3%, Chinese 11.2%, indigenous 3.4%, other 19.1%

Burma

307. What is the official name of Burma?
Union of Myanmar
308. When did the military government officially change the English translation of the country name from Burma to Myanmar?
June 18th, 1989
309. Which five countries still call the country Burma?
Australia, Canada, France, the United Kingdom and the United States
310. Which country borders Burma to the northeast?
China
311. Which country borders Burma to the southeast?
Thailand
312. Which country borders Burma to the east?
Laos
313. Which country borders Burma to the northwest?
India
314. Which country borders Burma to the west?
Bangladesh
315. Which body of water lies to the southwest of Burma?
Andaman Sea
316. Which body of water lies to the west of Burma?
Bay of Bengal

317. Burma includes which archipelago of over 800 islands in the Andaman Sea?
Mergui Archipelago (also called Myeik Archipelago and Myeik Kyunzu)

318. How large is the Cheduba Island (also called Manaung Island), located in the Bay of Bengal?
202 sq mi / 523 km²

319. The Coco Islands, located in Bay of Bengal, is geographically part of which archipelago?
Andaman Islands

320. Coco Islands is separated from the North Andaman Island (India) by which channel?
Coco Channel

321. Coco Islands consists of the main Great Coco Island and the smaller Little Coco Island, separated by which channel?

Alexandra Channel

322. What is the national anthem of Burma?
Till the End of the World, Burma

323. What is the capital of Burma?
Rangoon (also called Yangon, the largest city)

324. What is the second-largest city, which was the last royal capital of Burma?
Mandalay

325. What is the official language of Burma?
Burmese

326. What type of government does Burma have?
Military Regime

327. What was the First Anglo-Burmese War during March 5th, 1824 – February 24th, 1826?
The first war fought between the United Kingdom and the Konbaung Dynasty of Burma; Burma was forced to cede Assam, Manipur, Arakan and Tenasserim, lost influence in Cachar and Jaintia, and paid one million pounds sterling in indemnity

328. What was the result of the Second Anglo-Burmese War during April 5th, 1852 – January 20th, 1853?
British annexed the province of Pegu and renamed it Lower Burma

329. What was the result of Third Anglo-Burmese War during the winter of 1885?
British ended the Konbaung Dynasty in Upper Burma, and made it part of British India

330. When was Upper and Lower Burma united as Burma, within British India?
February 26th, 1886

331. When was Burma separated from British India to become a self-governing British colony?
April 1st, 1937

332. When did Burma gain independence from the United Kingdom?
January 4th, 1948

333. In which year did democratic rule in Burma end?
1962

334. What is the area of Burma?
261,159 sq mi / 676,578 km^2

335. How long is the coastline of Burma?
1,199 mi / 1,930 km

336. What is the population of Burma?
55,167,330 (by 2013)

337. What is the currency of Burma?
Kyat

338. What is the geographical feature of the terrain of Burma?
Central lowlands ringed by steep, rugged highlands

339. What is the highest point of Burma?
Hkakabo Razi (3,654 ft / 5,881m)

340. Hkakabo Razi is located in which mountain range?
Himalayas

341. Which mountain range forms the border between Burma and China?
Hengduan Shan Mountains

342. Which three mountain ranges in Burma run north-to-south from the Himalayas?

Rakhine Yoma, Bago Yoma, and Shan Plateau

343. What is the lowest point of Burma?
Andaman Sea (0 ft / 0 m)

344. What are major rivers in Burma?
Irrawaddy River, Salween River, Chindwin River, and Sittaung River

345. What is the longest river in Burma?
Irrawaddy River (also called Ayeyarwady River, 1,348 mi / 2,170 km)

346. What is the largest lake in Burma?
Indawgyi Lake

347. What are national parks in Burma?
Alaungdaw Kathapa National Park, Hlawga National Park, Khakaborazi National Park, Loimwe National Park, Mount Victoria National Park, and Popa Mountain National Park

348. What is the largest national park in Burma, located in Kachin state of Burma, which sourrounds Hkakabo Razi?
Khakaborazi National Park (1,472 sq mi / 3,812 km^2)

349. What is the second largest national park in Burma, located in Sagaing division of Burma, which is also a religious site that draws at least 30,000 pilgrims a year?
Alaungdaw Kathapa National Park (620 sq mi / 1,607 km^2)

350. What are administrative divisions called in Burma?
Divisions and states

351. How many divisions does Burma have?
7

352. How many states does Burma have?
7

353. What is the climate of Burma?
Tropical monsoon; cloudy, rainy, hot, humid summers (southwest monsoon, June to September); less cloudy, scant rainfall, mild temperatures, lower humidity during winter (northeast monsoon, December to April)

354. What are the natural resources of Burma?
Petroleum, timber, tin, antimony, zinc, copper, tungsten, lead, coal, marble, limestone, precious stones, natural gas, and hydropower

355. What are the natural hazards of Burma?
Destructive earthquakes and cyclones; flooding and landslides common during rainy season (June to September); periodic droughts

356. What are the religions of Burma?
Buddhist 89%, Christian 4% (Baptist 3%, Roman Catholic 1%), Muslim 4%, animist 1%, other 2%

357. What are the ethnic groups of Burma?
Burman 68%, Shan 9%, Karen 7%, Rakhine 4%, Chinese 3%, Indian 2%, Mon 2%, other 5%

Cambodia

358. What is the official name of Cambodia?
Kingdom of Cambodia

359. Which country borders Cambodia to the northwest?
   Thailand
360. Which mountain range forms a natural border between Cambodia and Thailand?
   Dângrêk Mountains
361. Which country borders Cambodia to the north?
   Laos
362. Which country borders Cambodia to the east and southeast?
   Vietnam
363. Which body of water lies to the Cambodia to the south?
   Gulf of Thailand
364. What is the motto of Cambodia?
   Nation, Religion, King
365. What is the national anthem of Cambodia?
   Royal Kingdom
366. What is the symbol of Cambodia?
   Angkor Wat, the Hindu temple complex at Angkor
367. What is the capital of Cambodia?
   Phnom Penh (the largest city)
368. What is the official language of Cambodia?
   Khmer
369. What type of government does Cambodia have?
   Multiparty Democracy under a Constitutional Monarchy
370. Which empire existed in Cambodia during 802 – 1431?
   Khmer (Angkor) Empire

371. Cambodia was parts of which countries?
Siam, Vietnam, and France
372. Cambodia became a protectorate of which country on August 11th, 1863?
France
373. When did Cambodia gain independence from France?
November 9th, 1953
374. When was the Cambodian monarchy abolished, and renamed the Khmer Republic?
October 9th, 1970
375. When did Cambodia become the Democratic Kampuchea, starting the Khmer Rouge age?
January 5th, 1976
376. What is the Khmer Rouge (also called Red Khmer)?
It was a name given to the followers of the Communist Party of Kampuchea, the totalitarian ruling party in Cambodia from 1975 to 1979
377. How many Cambodians died from execution, forced hardships, or starvation during the Khmer Rouge regime under Pol Pot?
More than 1.5 million
378. Which country occupied Cambodia on January 7th, 1979?
Vietnam
379. When did Cambodia become the State of Cambodia after Vietnamese occupation?
May 1st, 1989
380. During which period was Cambodia under the United Nations Transitional Authority in Cambodia (UNTAC) administration?
March 15th, 1992 – June 30th, 1993
381. When was the Kingdom of Cambodia restored?
September 24th, 1993
382. What is the area of Cambodia?
69,880 sq mi / 181,035 km^2
383. How long is the coastline of Cambodia?
275 mi / 443 km
384. What is the population of Cambodia?
15,205,539 (by 2013)
385. What are currencies of Cambodia?
Cambodian Riel and US Dollar
386. What is the geographical feature of the terrain of Cambodia?
Mostly low, flat plains; mountains in southwest and north
387. What is the highest point of Cambodia?
Phnum Aoral (5,938 ft / 1,810 m)
388. Phnum Aoral is located in which mountain range?
Cardamom Mountains
389. What is the lowest point of Cambodia?
Gulf of Thailand (0 ft / 0 m)
390. What is the longest river in Cambodia, located in China, Burma, Laos, Thailand, Cambodia, and Vietnam?
Mekong River (2,600 mi / 4,184 km)
391. What is the largest lake in Cambodia?

Tonlé Sap

392. The flow of Tonlé Sap changes direction twice a year. During the dry season, Tonlé Sap (about 1,042 sq mi / 2,700 km²) drains to a large river. During the rainy season, the river drains back to Tonlé Sap (about 6,176 sq mi / 16,000 km²). What is the name of the river?
Mekong River

393. Which national parks are located in Cambodia?
Bokor National Park, Botum-Sakor National Park, Kirirom National Park, Kep National Park, Phnom Kulen National Park, Ream National Park, and Virachey National Park

394. What is the largest national park in Cambodia, which is home to numerous species of wildlife?
Virachey National Park (1,284 sq mi / 3,325 km²)

395. What is the second largest national park in Cambodia, which is home to turtles, tortoises, elephants, tigers, bears, fishing cats and sea birds?
Botum-Sakor National Park (661 sq mi / 1,713 km²)

396. What is the third largest national park in Cambodia, which is famous for the Bokor Hill Station, built by the French in the 1920s to be used as a retreat from the heat of the plains?
Bokor National Park (also called Phnum Bokor National Park, Preah Monivong National Park, 541 sq mi / 1,400 km²)

397. What are administrative divisions called in Cambodia?
Provinces

398. How many provinces does Cambodia have?
23 (plus 1 municipality)

399. What is the climate of Cambodia?
Tropical; rainy, monsoon season (May to November); dry season (December to April); little seasonal temperature variation

400. What are the natural resources of Cambodia?
Oil and gas, timber, gemstones, iron ore, manganese, phosphates, and hydropower potential

401. What are the natural hazards of Cambodia?
Monsoonal rains (June to November); flooding; occasional droughts

402. What are the religions of Cambodia?
Buddhist 96.4%, Muslim 2.1%, other 1.3%, unspecified 0.2%

403. What are the ethnic groups of Cambodia?
Khmer 90%, Vietnamese 5%, Chinese 1%, other 4%

China

404. What is the official name of China?
People's Republic of China

405. Which countries border China to the northwest?
Kazakhstan and Kyrgyzstan

406. Which countries border China to the southwest?
India and Nepal

407. Which countries border China to the west?
Afghanistan, Pakistan, and Tajikistan

408. Which country borders China to the south?
Bhutan, Burma, Laos, and Vietnam

409. Which country borders China to the east?
North Korea

410. Which countries border China to the north?
Mongolia and Russia

411. Which body of water lies to the south of China?
South China Sea

412. Which bodies of water lie to the east of China?
East China Sea and Yellow China Sea

413. What is the motto of China?
Reform and open up

414. What is the national anthem of China?
March of the Volunteers

415. What is the capital of China?
Beijing

416. What is the largest city in China?
Shanghai

417. What is the official language of China?

Chinese

418. What type of government does China have?
Communist State

419. What is the Great Wall of China (5,500 mi / 8,852 km long)?
A series of stone and earthen fortifications in northern China, built originally to protect the northern borders of China against intrusions by various nomadic groups

420. What is the Northern Silk Road?
A prehistoric trackway in northern China originating in the early capital of Xi'an and extending north of the Taklamakan Desert to reach the ancient kingdoms of Parthia, Bactria and eventually Persia and Rome

421. What dynasties ruled China from 2852 BCE – 1911 CE?
Three Sovereigns and Five Emperors (2852 BCE – 2205 BCE), Xia Dynasty (2070 BCE – 1600 BCE), Shang Dynasty (1600 BCE – 1046 BCE), Zhou Dynasty (1045 BCE – 256 BCE), Qin Dynasty (221 BCE – 206 BCE), Han Dynasty (206 BCE – 220 CE), Three Kingdoms (220 – 280), Jin Dynasty (265 – 420), Southern Dynasty and Northern Dynasty (420 – 589), Sui Dynasty (581 – 618), Tang Dynasty (618 – 907), Five Dynasties and Ten Kingdoms (907 – 960), Song Dynasty (960 – 1279), Yuan Dynasty (1271 – 1368), Ming Dynasty (1368 – 1644), and Qing Dynasty (1644 – 1911)

422. What was the First Opium War (also called the First Anglo-Chinese War) during March 18th, 1839 – August 29th, 1842?
It was a war fought between the United Kingdom and China, with the aim of securing economic benefits from trade in China; it resulted in a British victory which opened up Chinese trade to the United Kingdom; China agreed to pay indemnities and ceded Hong Kong

423. What was the Taiping Rebellion during December 1850 – August 1864?
It was a widespread civil war in China, led by heterodox Christian convert Hong Xiuquan, against the ruling Qing Dynasty

424. What was the Second Opium War (also called the Second Anglo-Chinese War, the Second China War, the Arrow War, the Anglo-French expedition to China) during 1856 – 1860?
It was a war that the United Kingdom and France fought against China; it resulted in an Anglo-French victory, which opened more Chinese ports to Russia, the United States, the United Kingdom, and France; China also agreed to pay indemnities

425. What was the Boxer Rebellion, which occurred November 2nd, 1899 – September 7th, 1901?
It was an anti-colonialist, anti-Christian movement by the "Righteous Harmony Society"; the movement was crushed by Austria-Hungary, France, Germany, Italy, Japan, Russia, the United Kingdom, and the United States

426. What were main clauses in the Boxer Protocol, signed on September 7th, 1901, between the Qing Dynasty and the Eight-Nation Alliance plus Belgium, Spain and Netherlands?
China was to allow the foreign countries to base their troops in Beijing; China also agreed to pay indemnities

427. When was the Republic of China established?
January 1st, 1912

428. When was the People's Republic of China established?
October 1st, 1949

429. From December 8th, 1949, the Republic of China continued at which region?

34

Taiwan

430. What is the area of China?
3,705,407 sq mi / 9,596,961 km^2

431. How long is the coastline of China?
9,010 mi / 14,500 km

432. What is the population of China?
1,349,585,838 (by 2013)

433. What is China's rank by population in the world?
1st

434. What is the currency of China?
Renminbi

435. What is the geographical feature of the terrain of China?
Mostly mountains, high plateaus, deserts in west; plains, deltas, and hills in east

436. What is the highest point of China?
Mount Everest (29,035 ft / 8,850 m)

437. What is the lowest point of China?
Turpan Pendi (-505 ft / -154 m)

438. What is the longest river in China?
Yangtze River (3,915 mi / 6,300 km)

439. What is the Three Gorges Dam?
A hydroelectric dam on the Yangtze River; it is the largest electric dam in the world

440. Which river is the second longest river in China and is called "the cradle of Chinese civilization"?
Yellow River (3,395 mi / 5,464 km)

441. Which plateau covers an area of about 270,040 sq mi (640,000 km^2) in the upper and middle of China's Yellow River and Inner China?
Loess Plateau (also called Huangtu Plateau)

442. Which plain is based on the deposits of the Yellow River and is the largest alluvial plain of eastern Asia?
North China Plain

443. The southern part of North China Plain is traditionally referred to as what?
Central Plain

444. Which mountain range overlooks the North China Plain?
Taihang Mountains

445. What is the highest point of Taihang Mountains?
Xiao Wutaishan (9,455 ft / 2,882 m)

446. What is the third longest river in China, which rises in Nyang and flows into the South China Sea?
Pearl River (1,400 mi / 2,200 km)

447. Most of China's arable lands lie along which two rivers, which were the centers of China's major ancient civilizations?
Yangtze River and Yellow River

448. Which plateau in China is called the roof of the world?
Tibetan Plateau (also called Qinghai-Tibetan Plateau, Qingzang Plateau)

449. What is Tibetan Plateau's rank among plateaus by average elevation?

1st (Over 14,764 ft / 4,500 m)

450. What is Tibetan Plateau's rank among plateaus by area?
1st (about 965,000 sq mi / 2,500,000 km^2)

451. Which mountain range forms the northern edge of Tibetan Plateau?
Kunlun Mountains

452. What is the highest point of Kunlun Mountains?
Kunlun Goddess (23,514 ft / 7,167 m)

453. Which mountain range forms the northeastern edge of Tibetan Plateau?
Qilian Mountains

454. What is the highest point of Qilian Mountains?
Kangze'gyai (19,055 ft / 5,808 m)

455. Tibetan Plateau is transected by which river in south, which flows along the base of Himalayas?
Yarlung Tsangpo River (1,760 mi / 2,840 km)

456. Which lake, the largest in China, is at 10,515 feet (3,205 m) above sea level in a depression of Tibetan Plateau?
Qinghai Lake (1,733 sq mi / 4,489 km^2)

457. What is the highest point of Altun Mountains, between Kunlun Mountains Qilian Mountains?
Ak Tag (22,139 ft / 6,748 m)

458. What is the highest point of Tanggula Mountains in the central part of the Tibetan Plateau?
Purog Kangri (6929 m/22,733 ft)

459. What is the highest point of Gangdisi Mountains, located in Tibet Province?
Lunpo Gangri (23,278 ft / 7,095 m)

460. What is the highest point of Mount Nyainqêntanglha, located in Tibet Province?
Gyala Peri (23,930 ft / 7,294 m)

461. Which basin is more than 150,000 sq mi (400,000 km^2) in size, with the northern boundary at Tian Shan and the southern border at Kunlun Mountains?
Tarim Basin

462. Which desert dominates much of the Tarim Basin?
Taklamakan Desert (about 100,000 sq mi / 270,000 km^2)

463. What is the highest point of Greater Khingan Mountains, a volcanic mountain range in northeastern China?
6,677 ft / 2,035 m

464. Yungui Plateau (also called Yunnan-Guizhou Plateau) is located in which part of China?
Southwestern

465. Which mountain range provides a natural boundary between the North and South of China?
Qinling Mountains

466. What is the highest point of Qinling Mountains?
Mount Taibai (12,359 ft / 3,767 m)

467. Which mountain range provides a natural boundary between the central and south of China?
Nanling Mountains

468. Which canal in China is the longest canal in the world, starting at Beijing and ending in

Hangzhou?

Grand Canal (1,103 mi / 1,776 km)

469. How many national parks are there in China?

    225 (by 2013)

470. Which national parks are located in Beijin?

    Badaling- Shisanling National Park and Shihuadong National Park

471. Which national park includes the Great Wall of China?

    Badaling- Shisanling National Park

472. What is the national park located in Tianjin?

    Panshan National Park

473. Which national parks are located in Hebei?

    Chengde Bishushanzhuang Waibamiao National Park, Qinhuangdao Beidaihe National Park, Yeshanpo National Park, Cangyanshan National Park, Zhangshiyan National Park, Xibaipo - Tianguishan National Park, Taihang Daxiagu National Park, Xiangtangshan National Park, Wahuanggong National Park, and Kongshan Baiyundong National Park

474. Which national parks are located in Shanxi?

    Wutaishan National Park, Hengshan National Park, Qikou National Park, Huanghe Hukou Pubu National Park (trans-provincial), Beiwudangshan National Park, and Wulaofeng National Park

475. What is the national park located in Inner Mongolia?

    Zalantun National Park

476. Which national parks are located in Liaoning?

    Anshan Qianshan National Park, Yalujiang National Park, Jinshitan National Park, Xingcheng Haibin National Park, Dalian Haibin-Lushunkou National Park, Fenghuangshan National Park, Benxi Shuidong National Park, Qingshangou National Park, and Yiwulushan National Park

477. Which national parks are located in Jilin?

    Songhuahu National Park, "Badabu"-Jingyuetan National Park, Xianjingtai National Park, and Fangchuan National Park

478. Which national parks are located in Heilongjiang?

    Jingpohu National Park, Wudalianchi National Park, and Taiyangdao National Park

479. Which national parks are located in Jiangsu?

    Taihu National Park, Nanjing Zhongshan National Park, Yuntaishan National Park, Shugang Shouxihu National Park, and Sanshan National Park

480. Which national parks are located in Zhejiang?

    Hangzhou Xihu National Park, Fuchunjiang-Xin'anjiang National Park, Yandangshan National Park, Putuoshan National Park, Tiantaishan National Park, Shengsi Liedao National Park, Nanxijiang National Park, Moganshan National Park, Xuedoushan National Park, Shuanglong National Park, Xiandu National Park, Jianglangshan National Park, Xianju National Park, Huanjiang - Wuxie National Park, Fangyan National Park, Baizhangji - Feiyunhu National Park, Fangshan-Changyu Dongtian National Park, Dahongyan National Park, and Tianmushan National Park

481. How large is Hangzhou Xihu National Park, which is famous for its picturesque landscape, culture association with many scholars, national heroes and revolutionary martyrs, and many ancient buildings, stone caves and engraved tablets?

23 sq mi / 60 km^2

482. Which national parks are located in Anhui?

Huangshan National Park, Jiuhuashan National Park, Tianzhushan National Park, Langyashan National Park, Qiyunshan National Park, Caishi National Park, Chaohu National Park, Huashan Miku-Jianjiang National Park, Taijidong National Park, and Huatinghu National Park

483. What is the height of Huangshan, which is famous for its scenery, sunsets, peculiarly-shaped granite peaks, Huangshan Pine trees, and view of the clouds from above?

6,115 ft / 1,864 m

484. Which national parks are located in Fujian?

Wuyishan National Park, Qingyuanshan National Park, Gulangyu-Wanshishan National Park, Taimushan National Park, Taoyuandong-Linyin Shilin National Park, Taining National Park, Yuanyangxi National Park, Haitan National Park, Guanzhishan National Park, Gushan National Park, Yuhuadong National Park, Shibachongxi National Park, Qingyunshan National Park, Fozishan National Park, Baoshan National Park, Lingtongshan National Park, Meizhoudao National Park, and Fu'an Baiyunshan National Park

485. What is the height of Wuyishan, which is the largest and most representative example of Chinese subtropical forests and South Chinese rainforests' biodiversity?

7,080 ft / 2,158 m

486. Which national parks are located in Jiangxi?

Lushan National Park, Jinggangshan National Park, Sanqingshan National Park, Longhushan National Park, Xiannuhu National Park, Sanbaishan National Park, Meiling-Tengwangge National Park, Guifeng National Park, Gaoling-Yaoli National Park, Wugongshan National Park, Yunjushan-Zhelinhu National Park, Shennongyuan National Park, Damaoshan National Park, and Lingshan National Park

487. What is the height of Lushan, which is famous for the exceptional upthrows from the Quaternary age, amidst stunning landscapes: summits and peaks, valleys, gorges, gullies, rock formations, caves and waterfalls?

4,836 ft / 1,474m

488. Which national parks are located in Shandong?

Taishan National Park, Qingdao Laoshan National Park, Jiaodong Bandao Haibin National Park, Boshan National Park, and Qingzhou National Park

489. What is the height of the Taishan, which is the foremost of the "Five Sacred Mountains" and has historical and cultural significance in China?

5,029 ft / 1,533 m

490. Which national parks are located in Henan?

Jigongshan National Park, Luoyang Longmen National Park, Songshan National Park, Wangwushan-Yuntaishan National Park, Shirenshan National Park, Linlushan National Park, Qingtianhe National Park, Shennongshan National Park, Tongbaishan-Huaiyuan National Park, and Zhengzhou Huanghe National Park

491. Which national parks are located in Hubei?

Wuhan Donghu National Park, Wudangshan National Park, Changjiang Sanxia (also called Three Gorges)National Park (trans-provincial), Dahongshan National Park, Longzhong National Park, Jiugongshan National Park, and Lushui National Park

492. Which national parks are located in Hunan?

Hengshan National Park, Wulingyuan National Park, Yueyanglou Dongtinghu National Park, Shaoshan National Park, Yuelushan National Park, Langshan National Park, Mengdonghe National Park, Taohuayuan National Park, Ziquejie Titian-Meishan Longgong National Park, Dehang National Park, Suxianling-Wanhuayan National Park, Nanshan National Park, Wanfoshan-Dongzhai National Park, Huxingshan-Huayao National Park, Fenghuang National Park, Weishan National Park, Yandiling National Park, Baishuidong National Park, and Dongjianghu National Park

493. How large is Wulingyuan national park, which is famous for its approximately 3,100 tall quartzite sandstone pillars?
193 sq mi / 500 km^2

494. Which national parks are located in Guangdong?
Zhaoqing Xinghu National Park, Xiqiaoshan National Park, Danxiashan National Park, Baiyunshan National Park, Huizhou Xihu National Park, Luofushan National Park, Huguangyan National Park, and Wutongshan National Park

495. Which national parks are located in Guangxi?
Guilin Lijiang National Park, Guiping Xishan National Park, and Huashan National Park

496. What is the national park located in Hainan?
Sanya Redai Haibin National Park

497. Which national parks are located in Chongqing?
Changjiang Sanxia (also called Three Gorges) National Park (trans-provincial), Chongqing Jinyunshan National Park, Jinfoshan National Park, Simianshan National Park, Furongjiang National Park, Tanzhangxia National Park, and Tiankeng Difeng National Park

498. Which national parks are located in Sichuan?
Emeishan National Park, Huanglongsi-Jiuzhaigou National Park, Qingchengshan-Dujiangyan National Park, Jianmen Shudao National Park, Gongga Shan National Park, Shunan Zhuhai National Park, Xiling Xueshan National Park, Siguniangshan National Parks, Shihai Dongxiang National Park, Qionghai-Luojishan National Park, Bailonghu National Park Guangwushan-Nuoshuihe National Park, Tiantaishan National Park, and Longmenshan National Park

499. What is the height of Emeishan, which is the highest of the Four Sacred Buddhist Mountains of China and is famous for the Leshan Giant Buddha?
10,167 ft / 3,099 m

500. How large is Huanglongsi National Park, which is famous for diverse forest ecosystems, snow-capped peaks, waterfalls and hot springs, and is home to many endangered species including the Giant Panda and the Sichuan Golden Snub-nosed Monkey?
517 sq mi / 1,340 km^2

501. How large is Jiuzhaigou National Park, which is famous for its many multi-level waterfalls and colorful lakes?
278 sq mi / 720 km^2

502. Which national parks are located in Guizhou?
Huangguoshu National Park, Zhijindong National Park, Wuyanghe National Park, Hongfenghu National Park, Longgong National Park, Libo Zhangjiang National Park, Chishui National Park, Malinghe Xiagu National Park, Duyun Doupengshan-Jianjiang National Park, Jiudongtian National Park, Jiulongdong National Park, Liping Dongxiang National Park, Ziyun Getuhe Chuandong National Park, Pingtang National Park, Rongjiang Miaoshan Dongshui

National Park, Shiqian Wenquanqun National Park, Yanhe Wujiang Shanxia National Park, and Weng'an Jiangjiehe National Park

503. Which national parks are located in Yunnan?
Shilin National Park, Dali National Park, Xishuangbanna National Park, Sanjiang Bingliu National Park, Kunming Dianchi National Park, Lijiang Yulong Xueshan National Park, Tengchong Dire Huoshan National Park, Ruilijiang-Dayingjiang National Park, Jiuxiang National Park, Jianshui National Park, Puzhehei National Park, and Alu National Park

504. Which national parks are located in Tibet?
Yarlong He National Park, Nam Co-Nyainqêntanglha Shan National Park, Tulin - Gugê National Park, and Tanggula Shan-Nujiangyuan National Park

505. Which national parks are located in Shaanxi?
Huashan National Park, Lintong Lishan National Park, Huanghe Hukou Pubu National Park (trans-provincial), Baoji Tiantaishan National Park, Huangdiling National Park, and Heyang Qiachuan National Park

506. Which national parks are located in Gansu?
Maijishan National Park, Kongtongshan National Park, and Mingshashan-Yueyaquan National Park

507. What is the national park located in Qinghai?
Qinghaihu National Park

508. What is the national park located in Ningxia?
Xixia Wangling National Park and Xumishan Shiku National Park

509. Which national parks are located in Xinjiang?
Tianshan Tianchi National Park, Kumtag Shamo National Park, Bosten Hu National Park, Lop Ren Cunzhai National Park, and Sayram Hu National Park

510. What are administrative divisions called in China?
Provinces

511. How many provinces does China have?
23 (plus 5 autonomous regions and 4 municipalities)

512. What is the climate of China?
Extremely diverse; tropical in south to subarctic in north

513. What are the natural resources of China?
Coal, iron ore, petroleum, natural gas, mercury, tin, tungsten, antimony, manganese, molybdenum, vanadium, magnetite, aluminum, lead, zinc, uranium, and hydropower potential (world's largest)

514. What are the natural hazards of China?
Frequent typhoons (about five per year along southern and eastern coasts); damaging floods; tsunamis; earthquakes; droughts; land subsidence

515. What are the religions of China?
Daoist (Taoist), Buddhist, Christian 3%-4%, Muslim 1%-2%

516. What are the ethnic groups of China?
Han Chinese 91.5%, Zhuang, Manchu, Hui, Miao, Uyghur, Tujia, Yi, Mongol, Tibetan, Buyi, Dong, Yao, Korean, and other nationalities 8.5%

Cyprus

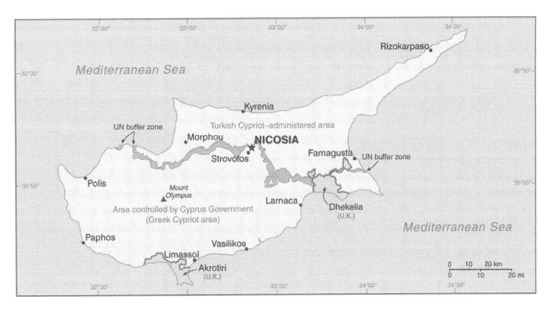

517. What is the official name of Cyprus?
    Republic of Cyprus
518. Turkey is at which direction of Cyprus?
    North
519. Syria and Lebanon are at which direction of Cyprus?
    East
520. What is the national anthem of Cyprus?
    Hymn to Liberty
521. What is the capital of Cyprus?
    Nicosia (also called Lefkosia, the largest city)
522. What are the official languages of Cyprus?
    Greek and Turkish
523. What type of government does Cyprus have?
    Republic
524. Cyprus has been occupied by which empires?

Hittite, Assyrian, Egyptian, Persian, Rashidun, Umayyad, Lusignan, Venetian and Ottoman

525. When did the United Kingdom administrate Cyprus under Ottoman suzerainty?
July 12th, 1878

526. When did the United Kingdom annex Cyprus?
November 5th, 1914

527. When did Cyprus gain independence from the United Kingdom?
August 16th, 1960

528. When did Turkey invade and occupy northern part of Cyprus?
July 15th, 1974

529. What is the area of Cyprus?
3,571 sq mi / 9,251 km^2

530. What is Cyprus' rank by size among islands in the Mediterranean Sea?
3rd

531. How long is the coastline of Cyprus?
403 mi / 648 km

532. What is the population of Cyprus?
1,155,403 (by 2013)

533. What is the currency of Cyprus?
Euro

534. What is the geographical feature of the terrain of Cyprus?
Central plain with mountains to north and south; scattered but significant plains along southern coast

535. What is the highest point of Cyprus, located in the Troodos National Forest Park (36 sq mi / 93 km²)?
Mount Olympus (6,401 ft / 1,951 m)

536. Mount Olympus is located in which mountain range?
Troodos Mountains

537. What is the lowest point of Cyprus?
Mediterranean Sea (0 ft / 0 m)

538. How many rivers are there in Cyprus?
35

539. What is the longest river in Cyprus?
Pedieos River (62 mi / 100 km)

540. What is the source of the Pedieos River?
Troodos Mountains

541. What is the mouth of the Pedieos River?
Famagusta Bay

542. What is the largest lake in Cyprus?
Limassol salt lake (4.1 mi / 11 km²)

543. What are administrative divisions called in Cyprus?
Districts

544. How many districts does Cyprus have?
6

545. What is the climate of Cyprus?
Temperate; Mediterranean with hot, dry summers and cool winters

546. What are the natural resources of Cyprus?
    Copper, pyrites, asbestos, gypsum, timber, salt, marble, and clay earth pigment
547. What are the natural hazards of Cyprus?
    Moderate earthquake activity; droughts
548. What are the religions of Cyprus?
    Greek Orthodox 78%, Muslim 18%, other (includes Maronite and Armenian Apostolic) 4%
549. What are the ethnic groups of Cyprus?
    Greek 77%, Turkish 18%, other 5%

Gaza Strip (Disputed)

 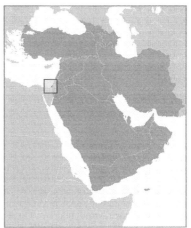

550. What is Gaza Strip's status?
    Israeli-occupied and the status is subject to the Israeli-Palestinian Interim Agreement
551. Which country borders Gaza Strip to the southwest?
    Egypt
552. Which country borders Gaza Strip to the south, east and north?
    Israel
553. What is the largest city of Gaza Strip?
    Gaza
554. What is the official language of Gaza Strip?
    Arabic
555. Who is in charge of the de facto government in Gaza Strip?
    Hamas
556. What is the area of Gaza Strip?

139 sq mi / 360 km^2

557. How long is the coastline of Gaza Strip?
25 mi / 40 km
558. What is the population of Gaza Strip?
1,763,387 (by 2013)
559. What are currencies of Gaza Strip?
Egyptian Pound and Israeli New Shekel
560. What is the geographical feature of the terrain of Gaza Strip?
Flat to rolling, sand- and dune-covered coastal plain
561. What is the highest point of Gaza Strip?
Abu 'Awdah (Joz Abu 'Auda, 344 ft / 105 m)
562. What is the lowest point of Gaza Strip?
Mediterranean Sea (0 ft / 0 m)
563. What is the climate of Gaza Strip?
Temperate, mild winters, dry and warm to hot summers
564. What are the natural resources of Gaza Strip?
Arable land and natural gas
565. What are the natural hazards of Gaza Strip?
Droughts
566. What are the religions of Gaza Strip?
Muslim (predominantly Sunni) 99.3%, Christian 0.7%
567. What are the ethnic groups of Gaza Strip?
Palestinian Arab

Georgia

568. Which country borders Georgia to the north?
Russia
569. Which country borders Georgia to the southeast?
Azerbaijan
570. Which countries border Georgia to the north?
Turkey and Armenia
571. Which body of water lies to the west of Georgia?
Black Sea
572. What is the motto of Georgia?
Strength is in Unity
573. What is the national anthem of Georgia?
Freedom
574. What is the capital of Georgia?
T'bilisi (the largest city)
575. What is the official language of Georgia?
Georgian
576. What type of government does Georgia have?
Unitary Semi-presidential Republic

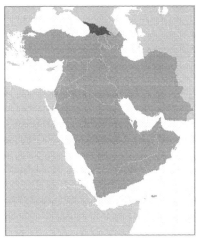

577. Georgia has been occupied by which empires?
Roman, Persian, Arabian Caliphate, Mongol, Ottoman and Russian

578. In 1491, Kingdom of Georgia was divided into which three Kingdoms?
Imertia, K'art'li, and Kakhet'i

579. When did Georgia sign the decree to be incorporated into Russian Emperor?
January 8th, 1801

580. When was the Democratic Republic of Georgia established?
May 26th, 1918

581. When was Georgian Soviet Socialist Republic established?
February 25th, 1921

582. When did Georgian gain independence from the Soviet Union?
April 9th, 1991

583. Which region declared independence from Georgia on November 28th, 1991?
South Ossetia (Republic of South Ossetia)

584. Which region declared independence from Georgia on July 23rd, 1992?
Abkhazia (Republic of Abkhazia)
585. Which country unilaterally recognized the independence of Abkhazia and South Ossetia on August 26th, 2008?
Russia
586. What is the area of Georgia?
26,916 sq mi / 69,700 km^2
587. How long is the coastline of Georgia?
193 mi / 310 km
588. What is the population of Georgia?
4,555,911 (by 2013)
589. What is the currency of Georgia?
Lari
590. What is the geographical feature of the terrain of Georgia?
Largely mountainous with Great Caucasus Mountains in the north and Lesser Caucasus Mountains in the south; Kolkhet'is Dablobi (Kolkhida Lowland) opens to the Black Sea in the west; Mtkvari River Basin in the east; good soils in river valley flood plains
591. What is the highest point of Georgia?
Mt'a Shkhara (17,064 ft / 5,201 m)
592. Mt'a Shkhara is located in which mountain range?
Greater Caucasus Mountains
593. What is the lowest point of Georgia?
Black Sea (0 ft / 0 m)
594. What is the longest river in Georgia, located in Turkey, Georgia, and Azerbaijan?
Mt'k'vari (also called Kura River, 941 mi / 1,515 km, Georgia: 270 mi / 435 km)
595. What cave in Georgia is the deepest cave in the world?
Voronya Cave (also called Krubera Cave, 7,188 ft / 2,191 m)
596. What are administrative divisions called in Georgia?
Regions
597. How many regions does Georgia have?
9 (plus 1 city, 2 autonomous republics)
598. What is the climate of Georgia?
Warm and pleasant; Mediterranean-like on Black Sea coast
599. What are the natural resources of Georgia?
Timber, hydropower, manganese deposits, iron ore, copper, minor coal and oil deposits; coastal climate and soils allow for important tea and citrus growth
600. What are the natural hazards of Georgia?
Earthquakes
601. What are the religions of Georgia?
Orthodox Christian 83.9%, Muslim 9.9%, Armenian-Gregorian 3.9%, Catholic 0.8%, other 0.8%, none 0.7%
602. What are the ethnic groups of Georgia?
Georgian 83.8%, Azeri 6.5%, Armenian 5.7%, Russian 1.5%, other 2.5%

Hong Kong (China)

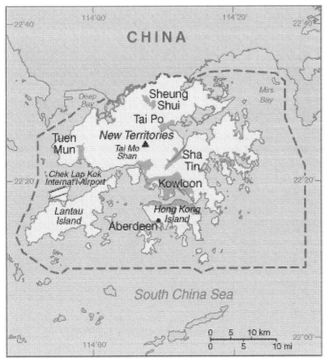

603. What is Hong Kong?
   A special administrative region of China

604. Hong Kong is at which direction of mainland China?
   South

605. Hong Kong is located in which body of water?
   South China Sea

606. Hong Kong is at the mouth of which river delta?
   Pearl River Delta

607. How many islands are there in Hong Kong?
   260

608. What are the official languages of Hong Kong?
   Chinese and English

609. When was Hong Kong ceded to the United Kingdom based on the Treaty of Nanking?
   August 29th, 1842

610. During which period was Hong Kong occupied by Japan?
   December 25th, 1941 – August 15th, 1945

611. When did Hong Kong become the Hong Kong Special Administrative Region of China?
   July 1st, 1997

612. What is the area of Hong Kong?
   426 sq mi / 1,104 km^2

613. How long is the coastline of Hong Kong?
   455 mi / 733 km

614. What is the population of Hong Kong?

7,182,724 (by 2013)
615. What is the geographical feature of the terrain of Hong Kong?
Hilly to mountainous with steep slopes; lowlands in north
616. What is the highest point of Hong Kong?
Tai Mo Shan (3,143 ft / 958 m)
617. What is the lowest point of Hong Kong?
South China Sea (0 ft / 0 m)
618. Hong Kong consists of which three main geographic territories?
Hong Kong Island, Kowloon Peninsula, and New Territories
619. What is the highest point of Hong Kong Island?
Victoria Peak (also called Mount Austin, or The Peak, 1,811 ft / 552 m)
620. New Territories comprises which areas?
Hong Kong mainland north of the Kowloon Ranges and south of the Sham Chun River, as well as the Outlying Islands
621. What is a natural landform harbor located between Hong Kong Island and Kowloon Peninsula?
Victoria Harbor
622. What is the climate of Hong Kong?
Subtropical monsoon; cool and humid in winter, hot and rainy from spring through summer, warm and sunny in fall
623. What are the natural resources of Hong Kong?
Outstanding deepwater harbor and feldspar
624. What are the natural hazards of Hong Kong?
Occasional typhoons
625. What are the religions of Hong Kong?
Eclectic mixture of local religions 90%, Christian 10%
626. What are the ethnic groups of Hong Kong?
Chinese 95%, Filipino 1.6%, Indonesian 1.3%, other 2.1%

India

627. What is the official name of India?
Republic of India
628. Which country borders India to the west?
Pakistan
629. Which countries border India to the east?
Bangladesh and Burma
630. Which countries border India to the north?
China, Nepal, and Bhutan
631. Which body of water lies to the west India?
Arabian Sea
632. Which body of water lies to the southeast of India?
Bay of Bengal
633. Which body of water lies to the south of India?
Indian Ocean

634. Sri Lanka and Maldives are in which direction of India?
South

635. Andaman and Nicobar Islands are in which direction of mainland India?
Southeast

636. How many islands are there in Andaman Islands (2,474 sq mi / 6,408 km^2)?
550 (26 inhabited)

637. How many islands are there in Nicobar Islands (711 sq mi / 1,841 km^2)?
22 (10 inhabited)

638. What is the motto of India?
Truth Alone Triumphs

639. What is the national anthem of India?
Thou Art the Ruler of the Minds of All People

640. What is the capital of India?
New Delhi

641. What is the largest city of India?
Mumbai

642. What are official languages of India?
Hindi and English

643. What type of government does India have?
Federal Constitutional Parliamentary Democracy

644. Which civilizations happened in India?
The Indus Valley civilization and the Vedic Civilization

645. What was the first empire that united much of the Indian subcontinent during 322 BCE – 185 BCE?

Mauryan Empire

646. Which empire brought the Golden Age of the flowering of Indian science, art, and culture during 240 – 550?
Gupta Empire

647. In the 10th and 11th centuries, Turks and Afghans invaded India and established which empire?
Delhi Sultanate

648. On May 27th, 1526, Emperor Babur established which empire that ruled India for more than three centuries?
Mughal Empire

649. What is Taj Mahal?
A mausoleum built by Mughal Emperor, Shah Jahan, in memory of his favorite wife, Mumtaz Mahal, during 1632 – 1653

650. What was East India Company during 1600 – 1857?
An early English joint-stock company that was formed initially for pursuing trade with the East Indies and ended up ruling the Indian subcontinent

651. What was the British Raj, which existed 1858 – 1947?
A British colony on the India subcontinent, including the present-day India, Pakistan, and Bangladesh

652. What were other areas under British Raj at various times?
Aden Colony (1858 – 1937), Lower Burma (1858 – 1937), Upper Burma (1886 – 1937), British Somaliland (1884 – 1898), and Singapore (1858 – 1867)

653. What was the capital of British Raj before it moved to New Delhi?
Calcutta

654. What was the currency of British Raj?
British Indian Rupee

655. Japan occupied which part of British Raj during March 1942 – August 1945?
Andaman Islands and Nicobar Islands

656. British Raj was split into India and Pakistan on what kind of basis?
Religious demographics

657. When did India gain independence from the United Kingdom?
August 15th, 1947

658. What is the area of India?
1,269,210 sq mi / 3,287,263 km^2

659. How long is the coastline of India?
4,350 mi / 7,000 km

660. What is the population of India?
1,220,800,359 (by 2013)

661. What is India's rank by population in the world?
2nd

662. What is the currency of India?
Indian Rupee

663. What is the geographical feature of the terrain of India?
Upland plain (Deccan Plateau) in south, flat to rolling plain along the Ganges, deserts in west, Himalayas in north

664. What is the highest point of India?
Kanchenjunga (28,209 ft / 8,598 m)

665. Kanchenjunga is located in which mountain range?
Himalayas

666. What is Kanchenjunga's rank by height in the world?
3rd

667. Which mountain range is situated near India's eastern border with Myanmar?
Patkai (also called Purvanchal)

668. Which mountain range runs across most of central India, which has a highest peak of Amarkantak (3,438 ft / 1,048 m)?
Vindhya

669. What is the highest point of Satpura Range in central India?
Dhupgarh (4,429 ft / 1,350 m)

670. What is the highest point of Aravalli Range in western India and eastern Pakistan?
Guru Shikhar (5,650 ft / 1,722 m)

671. What is the highest point of Western Ghats (also called Sahyadri Mountains) in western India?
Anamudi (8,842 ft / 2,695 m)

672. Eastern Ghats is a discontinuous range of mountains, which have been eroded and vivisected by which four major rivers in southern India?
Godavari, Mahanadi, Krishna, and Kaveri

673. What is the lowest point of India?
Indian Ocean (0 ft / 0 m)

674. What are major rivers in India?
Ganges River, Indus River, Beas River, Chenab River, Jhelum River, Ravi River, Sutlej River, Brahmaputra River, Narmada River, Tapi River, Godavari River, Krishna River, Kaveri River, and Mahanadi River

675. What is the longest river in India, located in India and Bangladesh?
Ganges River (1,560 mi / 2,510 km)

676. What is the largest lake in India?
Chilika Lake (brackish water, 450 sq mi / 1,165 km^2)

677. What are the 6 major islands in Chilika Lake?
Parikud, Phulbari, Berahpura, Nuapara, Nalbana, and Tampara

678. Which lake in India is the largest fresh water oxbow lake in Asia?
Kanwar Lake (26 sq mi / 68 km^2)

679. Which plain covers part of northwestern India?
Punjab Plain

680. Which plateau makes up the majority of the southern part of India?
Deccan Plateau (also called Great Peninsular Plateau)

681. About how large is the Thar Desert (also called Great Indian Desert), located in the northwestern Indian subcontinent?
77,000 sq mi (200,000 km^2)

682. What are Great Rann of Kutch and Little Rann of Kutch?
They are seasonal salt marshes located in the Thar Desert

683. How many exclaves of India are within Bangladeshi?

106

684. Which national parks are located in Jammu and Kashmir State?
Dachigam National Park, Kishtwar National Park, and Salim Ali National Park

685. Which national parks are located in Andaman and Nicobar Islands?
Campbell Bay National Park, Galathea National Park, Mahatma Gandhi Marine National Park, Middle Button Island National Park, Mount Harriet National Park, North Button Island National Park, Rani Jhansi Marine National Park, Saddle Peak National Park, and South Button Island National Park

686. Which national parks are located in Andhra Pradesh State?
Kasu Brahmananda Reddy National Park, Mahavir Harina Vanasthali National Park, Mrugavani National Park, and Sri Venkateswara National Park

687. Which national parks are located in Arunachal Pradesh State?
Mouling National Park and Namdapha National Park

688. Which national parks are located in Assam State?
Dibru-Saikhowa National Park, Kaziranga National Park, Manas National Park, Nameri National Park, and Orang National Park

689. Which national parks are located in Chhattisgarh State?
Indravati National Park, Kanger Ghati National Park, and Sanjay National Park (trans-state)

690. Which national parks are located in Gujarat State?
Vansda National Park, Blackbuck National Park, Gir National Park, and Gulf of Kachchh Marine National Park

691. Which national parks are located in Haryana State?
Kalesar National Park and Sultanpur National Park

692. Which national parks are located in Himachal Pradesh State?
Great Himalayan National Park and Pin Valley National Park

693. Which national parks are located in Jharkhand State?
Betla National Park and Hazaribag National Park

694. Which national parks are located in Karnataka State?
Anshi National Park, Bandipur National Park, Bannerghatta National Park, Kudremukh National Park, and Rajiv Gandhi National Park

695. Which national parks are located in Kerala State?
Eravikulam National Park, Mathikettan Shola National Park, Periyar National Park, and Silent Valley National Park

696. Which national parks are located in Madhya Pradesh State?
Bandhavgarh National Park, Fossil National Park, Kanha National Park, Madhav National Park, Panna National Park, Pench National Park, Satpura National Park, Van Vihar National Park, and Sanjay National Park (trans-state)

697. Which national parks are located in Maharashtra State?
Chandoli National Park, Gugamal National Park, Navegaon National Park, Pench National Park, Sanjay Gandhi National Park, and Tadoba National Park

698. Which national parks are located in Manipur State?
Keibul Lamjao National Park and Sirohi National Park

699. Which national parks are located in Meghalaya State?
Balphakram National Park and Nokrek National Park

700. Which national parks are located in Mizoram State?

Murlen National Park and Phawngpui Blue Mountain National Park

701. Which national parks are located in Orissa State?
Bhitarkanika National Park, Nandankanan National Park, and Simlipal National Park

702. Which national parks are located in Rajasthan State?
Darrah National Park, Desert National Park, Keoladeo National Park, Ranthambore National Park, and Sariska National Park

703. Which national parks are located in Tamil Nadu State?
Guindy National Park, Gulf of Mannar Marine National Park, Indira Gandhi National Park, Mudumalai National Park, and Mukurthi National Park

704. Which national parks are located in Uttarakhand State?
Corbett National Park, Gangotri National Park, Govind Pashu Vihar, Nanda Devi National Park, Rajaji National Park, and Valley of Flowers National Park

705. Which national parks are located in West Bengal State?
Gorumara National Park, Neora Valley National Park, Singalila National Park, and Sundarbans National Park

706. What are national parks, located in Goa State, Bihar State, Nagaland State, Sikkim State, and Uttar Pradesh State?
Mahaveer Sanctuary and Mollem National Park (Goa), Valmiki National Park (Bihar), Intaki National Park (Nagaland), Khangchendzonga National Park (Sikkim), Dudhwa National Park (Uttar Pradesh)

707. What is the oldest national park in India, which is a protected area for the critically endangered Bengal tiger of India?
Jim Corbett National Park (1936, 201 sq mi / 521 km^2)

708. What is the largest national park in India, which is located in Jammu and Kashmir State?
Hemis National Park (also called Hemis High Altitude National Park, 1,698 sq mi / 4,400 km^2)

709. What are administrative divisions called in India?
States

710. How many states does India have?
28 (plus 7 union territories)

711. What is the climate of India?
Varies from tropical monsoon in south to temperate in north

712. What are the natural resources of India?
Coal (fourth-largest reserves in the world), iron ore, manganese, mica, bauxite, titanium ore, chromite, natural gas, diamonds, petroleum, limestone, and arable land

713. What are the natural hazards of India?
Droughts; flash floods, as well as widespread and destructive flooding from monsoonal rains; severe thunderstorms; earthquakes

714. What are the religions of India?
Hindu 80.5%, Muslim 13.4%, Christian 2.3%, Sikh 1.9%, other 1.8%, unspecified 0.1%

715. What are the ethnic groups of India?
Indo-Aryan 72%, Dravidian 25%, Mongoloid and other 3%

Indonesia

716. What is the official name of Indonesia?
     Republic of Indonesia
717. Which countries share a land border with Indonesia?
     Papua New Guinea, Timor-Leste, and Malaysia
718. Singapore, Malaysia, Philippines are at which direction of Indonesia?
     North
719. Papua New Guinea is at which direction of Indonesia?
     East
720. Australia is at which direction of Indonesia?
     Southeast
721. How many islands are there in Indonesia?
     17,508 islands (about 6,000 inhabited)
722. What are the five main islands in Indonesia?
     Sumatra, Java, Borneo (also called Kalimantan, shared with Brunei and Malaysia), Sulawesi, and New Guinea (shared with Papua New Guinea)
723. What is the New Guinea's rank by size among islands in the world?
     2nd (303,381 sq mi / 2,130,800 km^2)

724. What is Borneo's rank by size among islands in the world?
    3rd (288,869 sq mi / 748,168 km^2)
725. What is Sumatra's rank by size among islands in the world?
    6th (171,069 sq mi / 443,066 km^2)
726. Sebatik Island, off the eastern coast of Borneo, is shared by Indonesia and which other country?
    Malaysia
727. What are two major archipelagos in Indonesia?
    Nusa Tenggara (also called Lesser Sunda Islands), and Maluku Islands (also called Moluccas, Moluccan Islands, or Spice Islands)
728. Which islands are located in Greater Sunda Islands and belong to or partially belong to Indonesia?
    Borneo (shared with Brunei and Malaysia), Java, Sumatra, and Sulawesi
729. Which islands are located in Lesser Sunda Islands and belong to or partially belong to Indonesia?
    Bali, Lombok, Sumbawa, Flores, Sumba, Timor (shared with Timor-Leste), Alor archipelago (shared with Timor-Leste), Barat Daya Islands, and Tanimbar Islands
730. What is the motto of Indonesia?
    Unity in Diversity
731. What is the national anthem of Indonesia?
    Great Indonesia
732. What is the capital of Indonesia?
    Jakarta (the largest city)
733. Jakarta is located on which island?
    Java
734. What is the official language of Indonesia?
    Indonesian
735. What type of government does Indonesia have?
    Unitary Presidential Republic
736. When was Dutch East India Company established to carry out colonial activities in Asia?
    March 20th, 1602
737. When was Dutch East Indies established at the present-day Indonesia?
    January 1st, 1800
738. When was Dutch East Indies occupied by Japan?
    March 8th, 1942 – September 29th, 1945
739. When did Indonesia gain independence from Netherlands?
    August 17th, 1945
740. When was Dutch East Indies renamed to Indonesia?
    September 20th, 1948
741. What is the area of Indonesia?
    735,164 sq mi / 1,904,569 km^2
742. How long is the coastline of Indonesia?
    33,999 mi / 54,716 km
743. What is the population of Indonesia?
    251,160,124 (by 2013)

744. What is Indonesia's rank by population in the world?
4th

745. What is Indonesia's rank by Muslim population in the world?
1st

746. What is the world's most populous island?
Java

747. What is the currency of Indonesia?
Rupiah

748. What is the geographical feature of the terrain of Indonesia?
Mostly coastal lowlands; larger islands have interior mountains

749. What is the highest point of Indonesia?
Puncak Jaya (also called Mount Carstensz or Carstensz Pyramid, 16,503 ft / 5,030 m)

750. Puncak Jaya is located in which mountain range?
Sudirman Mountains

751. Sudirman Mountains is located on which island?
New Guinea

752. What is Puncak Jaya's rank by height among island peaks in the world?
1st

753. What is the lowest point of Indonesia?
Indian Ocean (0 ft / 0 m)

754. Indonesia has numerous mountains and some 400 volcanoes. About how many volcanoes are active?
150

755. Which volcanic island had a huge eruption in 1883, which drastically altered the surrounding ocean floor as a result of the vast amount of the volcanic deposites?
Krakatoa (height: 2,667 ft / 813 m)

756. Which mountain is an active stratovolcano on Lesser Sunda Islands, whose 1815 outburst was the largest volcanic eruption by the ejecta volume in recorded history?
Mount Tambora (38 cu mi / 160 km^3, height: 8,930 ft / 2,722 m)

757. What is the death roll of 2004 Indian Ocean earthquake off the west coast of Sumatra on December 26th, 2004?
About 230,000

758. What is the largest lake in Indonesia?
Lake Toba (volcanic, 440 sq mi / 1,130 km^2)

759. Lake Toba is located on which island?
Sumatra

760. What are major rivers on Kalimantan?
Mahakam River, Martapura River, and Barito River

761. What are major rivers on Sumatra?
Asahan River, Hari River, and Musi River

762. What is the major river on Papua?
Baliem River

763. What are major rivers on Java?
Tarum River, Manuk River, Serang River, Serayu River, Solo River, and Brantas River

764. Which Indonesian national parks are located in Java?

Alas Purwo National Park, Baluran National Park, Bromo Tengger Semeru National Park, Gunung Ciremai National Park, Gunung Gede Pangrango National Park, Gunung Halimun National Park, Gunung Merapi National Park, Gunung Merbabu National Park, Karimunjawa National Park, Kepulauan Seribu National Park, Meru Betiri National Park, and Ujung Kulon National Park

765. Which Indonesian national parks are located in Kalimantan?
Betung Kerihun National Park, Bukit Baka Bukit Raya National Park, Danau Sentarum National Park, Gunung Palung National Park, Kayan Mentarang National Park, Kutai National Park, Sabangau National Park, and Tanjung Putting National Park

766. Which Indonesian national parks are located in Lesser Sunda Islands?
Bali Barat National Park, Gunung Rinjani National Park, Kelimutu National Park, Komodo National Park, Laiwangi Wanggameti National Park, and Manupeu Tanah Daru National Park

767. Which Indonesian national parks are located in Maluku and Papua?
Aketajawe-Lolobata National Park, Lorentz National Park, Manusela National Park, Teluk Cenderawasih National Park, and Wasur National Park

768. Which Indonesian national parks are located inn Sulawesi?
Bantimurung-Bulusaraung National Park, Bogani Nani Wartabone National Park, Bunaken National Park, Kepulauan Togean National Park, Lore Lindu National Park, Rawa Aopa Watumohai National Park, Taka Bone Rate National Park, and Wakatobi National Park

769. Which Indonesian national parks are located in Sumatra?
Batang Gadis National Park, Berbak National Park, Bukit Barisan Selatan National Park, Bukit Duabelas National Park, Bukit Tigapuluh National Park, Gunung Leuser National Park, Kerinci Seblat National Park, Sembilang National Park, Siberut National Park, Tesso Nilo National Park, and Way Kambas National Park

770. What is the largest national park in Indonesia, which contains a full altitudinal array of ecosystems spanning from marine areas, mangrove, tidal and freshwater swamp forest, lowland and montane rainforest, alpine areas, and equatorial glaciers?
9,674 sq mi / 25,056 km²

771. Puncak Jaya is located in which national park?
Lorentz National Park (9,672 sq mi / 25,056 km²)

772. What are administrative divisions called in Indonesia?
Provinces

773. How many provinces does Indonesia have?
30 (plus 2 special regions and 1 special capital city district)

774. What is the climate of Indonesia?
Tropical; hot, humid; more moderate in highlands

775. What are the natural resources of Indonesia?
Petroleum, tin, natural gas, nickel, timber, bauxite, copper, fertile soils, coal, gold, and silver

776. What are the natural hazards of Indonesia?
Occasional floods; severe droughts; tsunamis; earthquakes; volcanoes; forest fires

777. What are the religions of Indonesia?
Muslim 86.1%, Protestant 5.7%, Roman Catholic 3%, Hindu 1.8%, other or unspecified 3.4%

778. What are the ethnic groups of Indonesia?

Javanese 40.6%, Sundanese 15%, Madurese 3.3%, Minangkabau 2.7%, Betawi 2.4%, Bugis 2.4%, Banten 2%, Banjar 1.7%, other or unspecified 29.9%

Iran

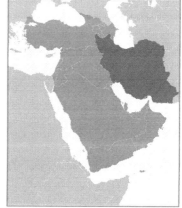

779. What is the official name of Iran?
     Islamic Republic of Iran
780. Which countries border Iran to the northwest?
     Armenia and Azerbaijan
781. Which countries border Iran to the west?
     Iraq and Turkey
782. Which countries border Iran to the northeast?
     Turkmenistan
783. Which countries border Iran to the east?
     Afghanistan and Pakistan
784. Which bodies of water lie to the south of Iran?
     Persian Gulf and the Gulf of Oman
785. Which body of water lies to the north of Iran?
     Caspian Sea
786. What is the motto of Iran?
     Independence, Freedom, Islamic Republic
787. What is the national anthem of Iran?
     National Anthem of the Islamic Republic of Iran
788. What is the capital of Iran?
     Tehran (the largest city)
789. What is the official language of Iran?

Persian

790. What type of government does Iran have?
Islamic Republic

791. What is Greater Iran (also called Greater Persia)?
It refers to the regions that have significant Iranian cultural influence; it roughly corresponds to the territory on the Iranian plateau, which consists of the area from the Euphrates River in the west to the Indus River and Syr Darya in the east and from Caucasus, Caspian Sea, and Aral Sea in the north to Persian Gulf and Gulf of Oman in the south

792. After centuries of foreign occupation and short-lived native dynasties, Iran was reunified as an independent state in 1501 by which empire?
Safavid Empire

793. What was the Anglo-Persian War, which occurred during November 1st, 1856 and April 4th, 1857?
It was a war between the United Kingdom and Iran over the city of Heart; it resulted with Iran ceding Heart to Afghanistan

794. The Russo-Persian Wars were a series of wars fought between the Russian Empire and Iran in the 18th and 19th centuries. What were the results of these wars?
Russian victories

795. Iran was occupied by the United Kingdom and Russia during January 10th, 1915 – August 8th, 1919. Which country withdrew in November 1917?
Russia

796. During which years was Iran a de facto British protectorate?
1919 – 1921

797. When was the English name "Persia" officially changed to Iran?
March 21st, 1935

798. Iran was occupied by which countries during August 25th, 1941 –March 2nd, 1946?
United Kingdom and Russia

799. When did Iran become an Islamic republic?
April 1st, 1979

800. What was the Iran–Iraq War (also called Imposed War, Holy Defense, Saddām's Qādisiyyah, or (First) Gulf War) during September 22nd, 1980 – August 20th, 1988?
It was a war between Iraq and Iran; it resulted in a great cost in lives and economic damage

801. What is the area of Iran?
636,372 sq mi / 1,648,195 km^2

802. How long is the coastline of Iran?
1,516 mi / 2,440 km

803. What is the population of Iran?
79,853,900 (by 2013)

804. What is the currency of Iran?
Rial

805. What is the geographical feature of the terrain of Iran?
Rugged, mountainous rim; high, central basin with deserts, mountains; small, discontinuous plains along both coasts

806. What is the highest point of Iran?
Kuh-e Damavand (18,606 ft / 5,671 m)

807. Kuh-e Damavand is located in which mountain range?
Alborz
808. What is Kuh-e Damavand's rank by height in Middle East?
1st
809. What is Kuh-e Damavand's rank by height among volcanoes in Asia?
1st
810. What is the lowest point of Iran?
Caspian Sea (-92 ft / -28 m)
811. Iran mostly lies on which plateau?
Iranian Plateau
812. What is the longest river in Iran?
Karun River (450 mi / 720 km)
813. What is the source of the Karun River?
Zard Kuh
814. What is the height of Zard Kuh, which is the highest peak of Zagros Mountains?
14,921 ft / 4,548m
815. What is the mouth of the Karun River?
Shatt al-Arab (also called Arvand Rud)
816. What is the largest lake in Iran?
Lake Urmia (about 2,000 sq mi / 5,200 km^2)
817. What is Lake Urmia's rank by size in the Middle East?
1st
818. What is Lake Urmia's rank by size among salt lakes in the world?
1st
819. What is the largest desert in Iran?
Dasht-e Kavir (also called Kavir-e Namak or Great Salt Desert, about 30,000 sq mi / 77,600 km^2)
820. Dasht-e Kavir, located in the middle of Iranian plateau, is what type of desert?
Salt desert
821. About how large is Dasht-e Lut, a salt desert located in southeastern Iran?
20,000 sq mi / 52,000 km^2
822. Which plain, mostly covered with marshes, was the center of the ancient Elamite culture of Iran?
Khuzestan Plain
823. Which plain is located in northern Iran?
Caspian Sea Coastal Plain
824. What is special about Ramsar, a coastal town next to of Caspian Sea?
Some areas around Ramsar have the highest level of natural radioactivity in the world, due to the presence of radioactive hot springs
825. Which national parks are located in Iran?
Golestan National Park, Sisangan National Park, Kavir National Park, Kharturan National Park, Tandooreh National Park, Khojir and Sorkhe Hesar National Park, Bakhtegan National Park, Lake Urmia National Park, Nazhvan Suburban Natural Park, and Bambo National Park
826. What is the oldest and largest national park in Iran?
Golestan National Park (355 sq mi / 919 km^2)

827. What are administrative divisions called in Iran?
Provinces

828. How many provinces does Iran have?
30

829. What is the climate of Iran?
Mostly arid or semiarid, subtropical along Caspian coast

830. What are the natural resources of Iran?
Petroleum, natural gas, coal, chromium, copper, iron ore, lead, manganese, zinc, and sulfur

831. What are the natural hazards of Iran?
Periodic droughts, floods; dust storms, sandstorms; earthquakes

832. What are the religions of Iran?
Muslim 98% (Shia 89%, Sunni 9%), other (includes Zoroastrian, Jewish, Christian, and Baha'i) 2%

833. What are the ethnic groups of Iran?
Persian 51%, Azeri 24%, Gilaki and Mazandarani 8%, Kurd 7%, Arab 3%, Lur 2%, Baloch 2%, Turkmen 2%, other 1%

Iraq

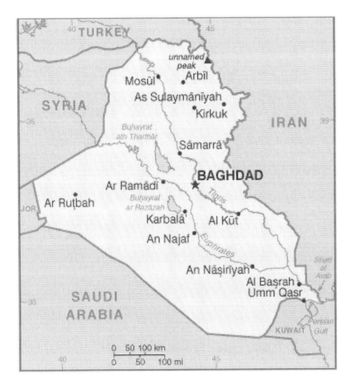

834. What is the official name of Iraq?
Republic of Iraq

835. Which country borders Iraq to the northwest?
Syria

836. Which country borders Iraq to the west?

Jordan
837. Which country borders Iraq to the north?
Turkey
838. Which country borders Iraq to the east?
Iran
839. Which country borders Iraq to the southeast?
Kuwait
840. Which country borders Iraq to the south?
Saudi Arabia
841. Which body of water lies to the southeast of Iraq?
Persian Gulf
842. What is the motto of Iraq?
God is Great
843. What is the national anthem of Iraq?
My Homeland
844. What is the capital of Iraq?
Baghdad (the largest city)
845. What is the official language of Iraq?
Arabic
846. What is official language in Kurdish regions?
Kurdish
847. What type of government does Iraq have?
Parliamentary Democracy
848. What are the two major rivers in Iraq?
Tigris River and Euphrates River
849. Which region in Iraq and part of neighboring countries is called the cradle of civilization?
Mesopotamia (Between the Tigris and Euphrates River)
850. What was the earliest known civilization with recorded history in Mesopotamia?
Sumer (6th millennium BCE – 3rd millennium BCE)
851. Iraq has been part of which empires?
Akkadian, Assyrian, Babylonian, Hellenistic, Parthian, Sassanid, Abbasid, Achaemenid, Roman, Rashidun, Umayyad, Mongol, Safavid, Afsharid, Ottoman and British empires
852. What was Mesopotamian campaign during November 1914 – November 14, 1918?
It was a campaign in Iraq fought between the United Kingdom, mostly from the Indian Empire, and the Central Powers, mostly of the Ottoman Empire
853. When did Iraq gain independence from the Ottoman Empire?
October 1st, 1919
854. When did Iraq become the League of Nations Mandate under the United Kingdom?
November 11th, 1920
855. When did Iraq gain independence from the League of Nations mandate under the United Kingdom?
October 3rd, 1932
856. What was the Anglo-Iraqi War during May 2nd, 1941 – May 31st, 1941?
A conflict between the United Kingdom and the rebel government of Rashid Ali; it was a British victory; the British supported Abdul Illah was restored

857. British forces remained in Iraq until which date?
October 26th, 1947
858. When did Iraq declare itself a republic?
July 14th, 1958
859. Iraq was in a war with which country during September 22nd, 1980 – August 20th, 1988?
Iran
860. What was the Iraq-Kuwait War (also called Invasion of Kuwait) during August 2nd, 1990 – August 4th, 1990?
It was a major conflict between Iraq and Kuwait, which resulted in Iraqi annexing Kuwait and triggering the Persian Gulf War
861. What was the Persian Gulf War during August 2nd, 1990 – February 28th, 1991?
It was a war waged by a the United Nations-authorized coalition force from 34 nations led by the United States and the United Kingdom against Iraq; It resulted in a coalition victory and the restoration of Kuwait
862. What was the 2003 invasion of Iraq March 20th, 2003 – May 1st, 2003?
The coalition force of the United States and the United Kingdom invaded Iraq and toppled the regime of Saddam Hussein
863. When did the Coalition Provisional Authority transfer sovereignty to the Iraqi-controlled Government?
June 28th, 2004
864. What is the area of Iraq?
169,234 sq mi / 438,317 km^2
865. How long is the coastline of Iraq?
36 mi / 58 km
866. What is the population of Iraq?
31,858,481 (by 2013)
867. What is the currency of Iraq?
Iraqi Dinar
868. What is the geographical feature of the terrain of Iraq?
Mostly broad plains; reedy marshes along Iranian border in south with large flooded areas; mountains along borders with Iran and Turkey; near the two major rivers are fertile alluvial plains
869. What is the highest point of Iraq?
Cheekha Dar (also called Black Tent, 11,847 ft / 3,611 m)
870. Cheekha Dar is located in which mountain range?
Zagros
871. What is the lowest point of Iraq?
Persian Gulf (0 ft / 0 m)
872. What are administrative divisions called in Iraq?
Governorates
873. How many governorates does Iraq have?
18 (plus 1 region)
874. What is the climate of Iraq?
Mostly desert; mild to cool winters with dry, hot, cloudless summers; northern mountainous regions along Iranian and Turkish borders experience cold winters with

occasionally heavy snows that melt in early spring, sometimes causing extensive flooding in central and southern Iraq

875. What are the natural resources of Iraq?
Petroleum, natural gas, phosphates, and sulfur
876. What are the natural hazards of Iraq?
Dust storms; sandstorms; floods
877. What are the religions of Iraq?
Muslim 97% (Shia 60%-65%, Sunni 32%-37%), Christian or other 3%
878. What are the ethnic groups of Iraq?
Arab 75%-80%, Kurdish 15%-20%, Turkoman, Assyrian, or other 5%

Israel

879. What is the official name of Israel?
State of Israel
880. Which country borders Israel to the north?
Lebanon
881. Which country borders Israel to the northeast?
Syria
882. Which country borders Israel to the east?
Jordan
883. Which country borders Israel to the southwest?
Egypt
884. Which body of water lies to the west of Israel?
Mediterranean Sea
885. Which body of water lies to the south of Israel?
Red Sea
886. What is the national anthem of Israel?
The Hope
887. What is the capital of Israel?
Jerusalem (the largest city)
888. Why does the international community not recognize Jerusalem as the capital of Israel?
Because Israel places most foreign embassies in Tel Aviv
889. What is the official language of Israel?
Hebrew
890. What are the official languages in Israel?
Hebrew and Arabic
891. What type of government does Israel have?
Parliamentary Democracy
892. When did Israel gain independence from the British Mandate of Palestine?
May 14th, 1948
893. What is the area of Israel?
8,522 sq mi / 22,072 km^2
894. How long is the coastline of Israel?
170 mi / 273 km

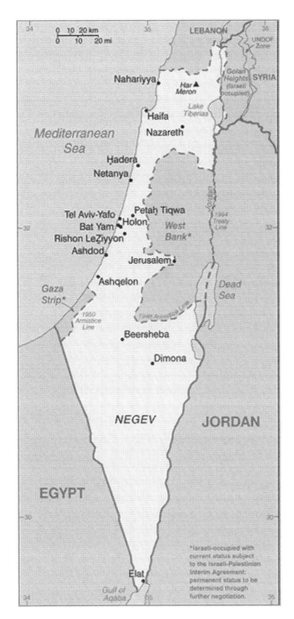

895. What is the population of Israel?
7,707,042 (by 2013)

896. What is the currency of Israel?
Shekel

897. What is the geographical feature of the terrain of Israel?
Negev desert in the south; low coastal plain; central mountains; Jordan Rift Valley

898. What is the highest point of Israel?
Mount Meron (3,963 ft / 1,208 m)

899. What is the highest point in Golan Heights, which is not recognized as part of Israel?
Mount Hermon (9,232 ft / 2,814 m)

900. How large is Golan Heights?

695 sq mi / 1,800 km^2

901. What is the lowest point of Israel?
Dead Sea (-1,339 ft / -408 m)

902. Which rocky desert, located in southern Israel, covers more than half of Israel?
Negev Desert (also called al-Naqab)

903. Which craterlike geological erosional landform is unique for the Negev Desert?
Makhtesh

904. What is the world's largest makhtesh, located at the peak of Mount Negev, which is a valley surrounded by steep walls and drained by a single riverbed, Saharonim Spring?
Makhtesh Ramon (100 sq mi / 160 km^2)

905. What is the second largest makhtesh in Israel, which is drained by the Nahal Hatira River?
HaMakhtesh HaGadol (23 sq mi / 60 km^2)

906. The most holy places of Judaism, such as Temple Mount and Tomb of the Patriarchs, are located in which mountain range?
Judean Mountains, (also called Judean Hills, Hebron Hills, or Jibal al-Khalil)

907. Israeli Coastal Plain is the narrow coastal plain along Israel's Mediterranean Sea coast which includes about what percentage of the population?
70%

908. Which coastal mountain range in northern Israel stretches from Mediterranean Sea towards the southeast?
Mount Carmel (1,724 ft / 525.4 m)

909. What is the largest lake in Israel?
Sea of Galilee (freshwater, 64 sq mi / 166 km^2)

910. What is the Sea of Galilee's rank by elevation among world's lakes?
Second lowest (-686 ft / -209 m)

911. What is the Sea of Galilee's rank by elevation among world's fresh lakes?
Lowest

912. What are inflows of the Sea of Galilee?
Upper Jordan River and local runoff

913. What is outflow of the Sea of Galilee?
Lower Jordan River

914. The Jordan River is located in which valley?
Jordan Rift Valley

915. What is the longest river in Israel?
Jordon River (156 mi / 251 km)

916. How many Israeli civilian sites are located in West Back?
100

917. How many Israeli civilian sites are located in Golan Heights?
42

918. What are administrative divisions called in Israel?
Districts

919. How many districts does Israel have?
6

920. Which national parks are located in Israel?
Akhziv Beach National Park, Alexander River National Park, Ashkelon National Park, Avdat

National Park, Arbel National Park and Nature Reserve, Bar'am National Park, Beit Alfa Synagogue National Park, Beit Guvrin National Park, Beit She'an National Park, Beit She'arim National Park, Caesarea National Park, Castel National Park, Cochav Hayarden National Park, Korazim National Park, National Park at Prime Minister David Ben-Gurion's Grave, Ein Avdat National Park, Ein Gedi Antiquities National Park, Ein Hemed National Park, Eshkol National Park, Gan Hashlosha National Park, Hamat Tiberias National Park, Harod Spring National Park, Herodion National Park, Hermon National Park, Kursi National Park, Hurshat Tal National Park, Mamshit National Park, Masada National Park, Mount Carmel National Park, Nimrod Fortress National Park, Qumran National Park, Ramon Park Complex, Sharon National Park, Shivta National Park, Shomron National Park, Tel Arad National Park, Tel Be'er Sheva National Park, Tel Hazor National Park, Tel Megiddo National Park, Yarkon National Park, Yehi'am Fortress National Park, and Zippori National Park

921. Which national parks are located in Golan Heights?
Hermon National Park, Kursi National Park, and Nimrod Fortress National Park

922. Which national parks are located in West Bank?
Herodion National Park, Qumran National Park, and Shomron National Park

923. What is the largest national park in Israel, located in northern Israel, which is famous for its wild cliffs and green landscapes?
Mount Carmel National Park (210 km^2)

924. What is the climate of Israel?
Temperate; hot and dry in southern and eastern desert areas

925. What are the natural resources of Israel?
Timber, potash, copper ore, natural gas, phosphate rock, magnesium bromide, clays, and sand

926. What are the natural hazards of Israel?
Sandstorms may occur during spring and summer; droughts; periodic earthquakes

927. What are the religions of Israel?
Jewish 76.4%, Muslim 16%, Arab Christians 1.7%, other Christian 0.4%, Druze 1.6%, unspecified 3.9%

928. What are the ethnic groups of Israel?
Jewish 76.4% (of which Israel-born 67.1%, Europe/America-born 22.6%, Africa-born 5.9%, Asia-born 4.2%), non-Jewish 23.6% (mostly Arab)

Japan

929. What is the official name of Japan?
State of Japan

930. China and Korea are at which direction of Japan?
West

931. Russia is at which direction of Japan?
Southeast

932. How many islands are there in Japan?
6,852

933. What are the four main islands in Japan, together accounting for 97% of Japan's land area?
Honshu (88,017 sq mi / 227,963 km^2), Hokkaido (32,213 sq mi / 83,454 km²), Kyushu (13,761 sq mi / 35,640 km^2) and Shikoku (7,260 sq mi / 18,800 km^2)

934. Which sea has almost 3,000 islands, and is the body of water separating Honshu, Shikoku, and Kyushu?
Inland Sea

935. What is the national anthem of Japan?
Kimigayo

936. What is the capital of Japan?
Tokyo (the largest city)

937. What is the official language of Japan?
Japanese

938. What type of government does Japan have?
Constitutional Monarchy with Parliamentary Democracy

939. When was Japan founded by the ancestral Emperor Jimmu according to Japanese mythology?
February 11th, 660 BCE

940. When was the country named Nippon?
January 22nd, 646

941. When was the shogunate (a military-led, dynastic government) established?
August 21st, 1192

942. What was the name of the long period of relative political stability and flowering of

Japanese indigenous culture during February 12th, 1603 – November 9th, 1867?
Edo period (also called Tokugawa period)

943. What was the Boshin War during January 1868 – May 1869?
It was a civil war in Japan, which ended the shogunate and restored the imperial rule; the war was the military phase of the Meiji Restoration

944. What was the First Sino-Japanese War during August 1st, 1894 – April 17th, 1895
A war fought between China and Japan primarily over control of Korea, Manchuria, Taiwan, and Yellow Sea; it was a Japanese victory; Korea becomes independent from China; China ceded Taiwan, Penghu, and Liaodong Peninsula to Japan

945. What was the Russo-Japanese War during February 8th, 1904 – September 5th, 1905?
A war fought between Russian and Japan over Manchuria and Korea at Manchuria and Yellow Sea; it was a Japanese victory; Treaty of Portsmouth was signed, from which both Japan and Russia agreed to evacuate Manchuria and return its sovereignty to China, but Japan was leased the Liaodong Peninsula (containing Port Arthur and Talien) and the Russian rail system in southern Manchuria with access to strategic resources; Japan also received the southern half of the Island of Sakhalin from Russia

946. Japan annexed which country during August 28th, 1910 – Sep 12th, 1945?
Korea

947. After World War I, Japan joined the League of Nations and received a mandate over Pacific islands north of the Equator formerly held by which country?
Germany

948. What was the Second Sino-Japanese War during July 7th, 1937 – September 9th, 1945?
A military conflict fought between China and Japan at China; it ended with the unconditional surrender of all Japanese forces in mainland China; China reclaimed and took control of Taiwan and Penghu

949. During World War II, Japan invaded China, and conquered which areas in Asia?
French Indochina (Vietnam, Laos, and Cambodia), British Malaya (Brunei, Malaysia, and Singapore), Dutch East Indies (Indonesia), and Burma

950. What were the consequences of the Japanese attack on the United States naval base at Pearl Harbor, Hawaii, on December 7th, 1941?
Japanese major tactical victory; the United States declared war on Japan; Germany and Italy declared war on the United States

951. The United States atomic bombs were dropped on which two cities in Japan?
Hiroshima (August 6th, 1945) and Nagasaki (August 9th, 1945)

952. When did Japan announce its surrender to the Allied Powers?
August 15th, 1945

953. When did a 9.0 earthquake occur in Japan, triggering tsunamis and disabling the Fukushima nuclear facility, resulting in thousands dead and the biggest nuclear crisis since Chernobyl?
March 11th, 2011

954. When was the Instrument of Surrender signed, which officially ended the Pacific War and therefore World War II?
September 2nd, 1945

955. Who occupied Japan during September 2nd, 1945 – April 28th, 1952?
Allied

956. What is the area of Japan?

145,879 sq mi / 377,915 km^2

957. How long is the coastline of Japan?
18,286 mi / 29,751 km

958. What is the population of Japan?
127,253,075 (by 2013)

959. What is the currency of Japan?
Yen

960. What is the geographical feature of the terrain of Japan?
Mostly rugged and mountainous

961. What is the highest point of Japan?
Mount Fuji (active stratovolcano, 12,389 ft / 3,776 m)

962. Mount Fuji and which two other mountains are Japan's "Three Holy Mountains"?
Mount Tate (9,892 ft / 3,015 m) and Mount Haku (8,865 ft / 2,702.2 m)

963. What is the largest plain in Japan?
Kanto Plain (12,519 sq mi / 32,424 km^2)

964. What is the lowest point of Japan?
Hachiro-gata (-13 ft / -4 m)

965. What is Hachiro-gata's rank by size among Japanese lakes?
2nd (19 sq mi / 48 km²)

966. What is the largest lake in Japan?
Lake Biwa (182 sq mi / 470 km²)

967. What is the primary outflow of Lake Biwa?
Seta River (120 mi / 75 km)

968. What is the longest river in Japan, which flows from Nagano Prefecture to Niigata Prefecture?
Shinano River (228 mi / 367 km)

969. Which canal was built to defend Niigata from floods in 1922?
Okozu Canal

970. What are Bonin Islands (also called Ogasawara Group)?
An archipelago of over 30 subtropical and tropical islands, directly south of Tokyo

971. What are three islands in Daito Islands?
Kita Daito-jima (5 sq mi / 13 km²), Minami Daito-jima (12 sq mi / 31 km²), Oki Daito-jima (0.4 sq mi / 1.1 km²)

972. Which island is the easternmost territory in Japan?
Minami Torishima (also called Marcus Island, 0.5 sq mi / 1.2 km²)

973. Which atoll is the southernmost island in Japan?
Okinotorishima

974. Which Japanese island chain lies in the East China Sea and consists of about 100 islands,
Ryuku Islands

975. What are three islands in Volcano Islands, which lies south of the Bonin Islands?
North Iwo Jima (2.2 sq mi / 5.6 km^2), Iwo Jima (8 sq mi / 21 km^2), and South Iwo Jima (1.3 sq mi / 3.4 km²)

976. What are national parked located in Japan?
Rishiri-Rebun-Sarobetsu National Park, Shiretoko National Park, Daisetsuzan National Park, Akan National Park, Kushiro Shitsugen National Park, Shikotsu-Toya National Park, Towada-

Hachimantai National Park, Rikuchu Kaigan National Park, Bandai-Asahi National Park, Nikko National Park, Oze National Park, Chichibu-Tama-Kai National Park, Joshinetsu Kogen National Park, Ogasawara National Park, Fuji-Hakone-Izu National Park, Chubu Sangaku National Park, Hakusan National Park, Minami Alps National Park, Ise-Shima National Park, Yoshino-Kumano National Park, Sanin Kaigan National Park, Daisen-Oki National Park, Setonaikai National Park, Ashizuri-Uwakai National Park, Saikai National Park, Unzen-Amakusa National Park, Aso-Kuju National Park, Kirishima-Yaku National Park, and Iriomote-Ishigaki National Park

977. What is the largest national park in Japan, located on Hokkaido, which has 16 mountain peaks over 6,562 ft (2,000 m), 3 volcanic mountain groups, and many hot springs?
Daisetsuzan National Park (875 sq mi / 2,268 km²)

978. What is the second largest national park in Japan, located on Honshu, which has a number of volcanoes including Mount Asama, Mount Myoko and Mount Tanigawa?

979. Joshinetsu Kogen National Park (730 sq mi / 1,891 km²)
What is the third largest national park in Japan, located on Honshu, which has many mountain peaks?
Bandai-Asahi National Park (722 sq mi / 1,870 km²)

980. What are administrative divisions called in Japan?
Prefectures

981. How many prefectures does Japan have?
47

982. What is the climate of Japan?
Varies from tropical in south to cool temperate in north

983. What are the natural resources of Japan?
Negligible mineral resources and fish

984. What are the natural hazards of Japan?
Many dormant and some active volcanoes; about 1,500 seismic occurrences (mostly tremors) every year; tsunamis; typhoons

985. What are the religions of Japan?
Shintoism 83.9%, Buddhism 71.4%, Christianity 2%, other 7.8%

986. What are the ethnic groups of Japan?
Japanese 98.5%, Koreans 0.5%, Chinese 0.4%, other 0.6%

Jordan

987. What is the official name of Jordan?
Hashemite Kingdom of Jordan

988. Which country borders Jordan to the southeast?
Saudi Arabia

989. Which country borders Jordan to the east?
Iraq

990. Which country borders Jordan to the north?
Syria

991. Which country borders Jordan to the west?
Israel

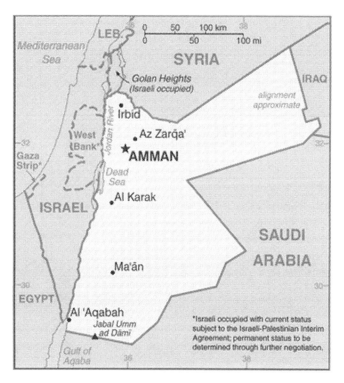

992. The 16 mi (26 km) long shoreline along the Gulf of Aqaba provides Jordan's access to which body of water?
Red Sea

993. What is the motto of Jordan?
God, The Homeland, The King

994. What is the national anthem of Jordan?
The Royal Anthem of Jordan

995. What is the capital of Jordan?
Amman (the largest city)

996. What is the official language of Jordan?
Arabic

997. What type of government does Jordan have?
Constitutional Monarchy

998. What was Jordan's name when the Semitic Amorites settled around the Jordan River at around 2000 BCE?
Canaan

999. Which empires have invaded or settled in Jordan before the British occupation on September 25th, 1918?
Hittites, Egyptians, Israelites, Assyrians, Babylonians, Persians, Greeks, Romans, Arab Muslims, Seljuks, Christian Crusaders, Eyyubids, Mongols, Mameluks, Ottoman Turks, and Circassians

1000. When did Jordan gain independence from the British Mandate of Palestine?
May 25th, 1946

1001. Which area did Jordan relinquish its claim on July 31st, 1988?

West Bank
1002. What is the area of Jordan?
34,486 sq mi / 89,342 km^2
1003. How long is the coastline of Jordan?
16 mi / 26 km
1004. What is the population of Jordan?
6,482,081 (by 2013)
1005. What is the currency of Jordan?
Jordanian Dinar
1006. What is the geographical feature of the terrain of Jordan?
Mostly desert plateau in east, highland area in west; Great Rift Valley separates East and West Banks of the Jordan River
1007. What is the highest point of Jordan?
Jabal Umm ad Dami (6,083 ft / 1,854 m)
1008. What is the lowest point of Jordan?
Dead Sea (-1,339 ft / -408 m)
1009. What is the longest river in Jordan, located in Israel and Jordon?
Jordon River (156 mi / 251 km)
1010. What are administrative divisions called in Jordan?
Governorates
1011. How many governorates does Jordan have?
12
1012. What is the climate of Jordan?
Mostly arid desert; rainy season in west (November to April)
1013. What are the natural resources of Jordan?
Phosphates, potash, and shale oil
1014. What are the natural hazards of Jordan?
Droughts; periodic earthquakes
1015. What are the religions of Jordan?
Sunni Muslim 92%, Christian 6% (majority Greek Orthodox, but some Greek and Roman Catholics, Syrian Orthodox, Coptic Orthodox, Armenian Orthodox, and Protestant denominations), other 2% (several small Shia Muslim and Druze populations)
1016. What are the ethnic groups of Jordan?
Arab 98%, Circassian 1%, Armenian 1%

Kazakhstan

1017. What is the official name of Kazakhstan?
Republic of Kazakhstan
1018. Which country borders Kazakhstan to the southeast?
China
1019. Which countries border Kazakhstan to the south?
Turkmenistan, Uzbekistan, and Kyrgyzstan
1020. Which country borders Kazakhstan to the north and west?
Russia

1021. Which body of water lies to the southwest of Kazakhstan?
Caspian Sea

1022. Which region of Kazakhstan geographically belongs in Europe?
The region east of the Ural River

1023. What is the national anthem of Kazakhstan?
My Kazakhstan

1024. What is the capital of Kazakhstan?
Astana

1025. What is the largest city of Kazakhstan?
Almaty

1026. What are the official languages of Kazakhstan?
Russian and Kazakh

1027. What type of government does Kazakhstan have?
Presidential Republic

1028. Kazakhstan was annexed by which empire during 1731 – 1917?
Russian

1029. When was the Kirghiz Autonomous Soviet Socialist Republic established?
August 26th, 1920

1030. When did Kazakhstan gain independence from the Soviet Union?
December 16th, 1991

1031. What is the area of Kazakhstan?
1,052,085 sq mi / 2,724,900 km^2

1032. What is Kazakhstan's rank by size among landlocked countries in the world?
1st

1033. How long is the coastline of Kazakhstan?
0 mi / 0 km (landlocked)

1034. What is the population of Kazakhstan?
17,736,896 (by 2013)

1035. What is the currency of Kazakhstan?
Tenge

1036. What is the geographical feature of the terrain of Kazakhstan?
Vast flat steppe extending from the Volga in the west to the Altai Mountains in the east and from the plains of western Siberia in the north to oases and deserts of Central Asia in the south

1037. What is the highest point of Kazakhstan?
Khan Tangiri (22,950 ft / 6,995 m)

1038. Khan Tangiri is located in which mountain range?
Tian Shan

1039. Khan Tangiri is on the Kazakhstan border with which countries?
China and Kyrgyzstan

1040. What is the lowest point of Kazakhstan?
Vpadina Kaundy (also called Karagiye Depression, -433 ft / -132 m)

1041. How many rivers are more than 62 mi (100 km) long in Kazakhstan?
155

1042. What are major rivers in Kazakhstan?
Irtysh River, Ural River, Chu River, and Syr Darya

1043. What is the longest river in Kazakhstan, located in Russia, Kazakhstan, China, and Mongolia?
Irtysh (also called Ertys, 2,640 mi / 4,248 km, Kazakhstan: 1,056 mi / 1,700 km)

1044. What is the largest lake in Kazakhstan?
Lake Balkhash (endorheic and saline, 7,115 sq mi / 18,428 km^2)

1045. What are primary inflows of Lake Balkhash?
Ili River, Karatal River, Aksu River, Lepsi River, Byan River, Kapal River, and Koksu River

1046. Kazakhstan shared the Aral Sea with which country?
Uzbekistan

1047. What type of lake is the Aral Sea?
Endorheic and Saline

1048. What are primary inflows of the Aral Sea?
Amu Darya and Syr Darya

1049. How large was the Aral Sea in 1960?
26,000 sq mi / 68,000 km^2

1050. How large was the Aral Sea in 1998 when it split into two lakes (North Aral Sea and South

Aral Sea)?

11,076 sq mi / 28,687 km^2

1051. How large was the Aral Sea in 2004 after South Aral Sea split into Eastern Sea and Western Sea (three lakes)?

6,630 sq mi / 17,160 km^2

1052. By 2009, which part of the Aral Sea disappeared?

Eastern Sea

1053. How large is the Lake Zaysan, a freshwater lake in eastern Kazakhstan?

700 sq mi / 1,810 km²

1054. Which national parks are located in Kazakhstan?

Altyn-Emel National Park, Bayanaul National Park, Burabay National Park, Charyn National Park, Ile-Alatau National Park, Karkaraly National Park, Katon-Karagay National Park, Kokshetau National Park, Kolsay Lakes National Park, and Sayram-Ugam National Park

1055. What is the largest national park, located in eastern Kazakhstan, which is famous for snow covered mountain peaks, fantastical rocky cliffs, enchanting cedar forests, wonderful lakes, fast-flowing rivers and brightly colored wildflowers?

Katon-Karagay National Park (2,484 sq mi / 6,435 km²)

1056. What is the second largest national park, located between the Ili River and the Ak-Tau mountain range, which is famous for the singing sand?

Altyn-Emel National Park (1,776 sq mi / 4,600 km^2)

1057. What is the third largest national park, located in southeastern Kazakhstan, which stretches from the magnificent Turgen Gorge in the east, to the Chemolgan River in the west?

Ile-Alatau National Park (781 sq mi / 2,023 km²)

1058. What are administrative divisions called in Kazakhstan?

Provinces

1059. How many provinces does Kazakhstan have?

14

1060. What is the climate of Kazakhstan?

Continental, cold winters and hot summers, arid and semiarid

1061. What are the natural resources of Kazakhstan?

Major deposits of petroleum, natural gas, coal, iron ore, manganese, chrome ore, nickel, cobalt, copper, molybdenum, lead, zinc, bauxite, gold, and uranium

1062. What are the natural hazards of Kazakhstan?

Earthquakes in the south; mudslides around Almaty

1063. What are the religions of Kazakhstan?

Muslim 47%, Russian Orthodox 44%, Protestant 2%, other 7%

1064. What are the ethnic groups of Kazakhstan?

Kazakh (Qazaq) 53.4%, Russian 30%, Ukrainian 3.7%, Uzbek 2.5%, German 2.4%, Tatar 1.7%, Uyghur 1.4%, other 4.9%

Korea, North

1065. What is the official name of North Korea?

Democratic People's Republic of Korea

1066. Which country borders North Korea to the north and northwest?
China

1067. Which country borders North Korea to the northeast?
Russia

1068. Which country borders North Korea to the south?
South Korea

1069. Which bodies of water lie to the west of North Korea?
Yellow Sea and Korea Bay

1070. Which body of water lies to the east of North Korea?
Sea of Japan

1071. What is the motto of North Korea?
Powerful and Prosperous Nation

1072. What is the national anthem of North Korea?
The Patriotic Song

1073. What is the capital of North Korea?
Pyongyang (the largest city)

1074. What is the official language of North Korea?
Korean

1075. What type of government does North Korea have?
Communist state one-man dictatorship

1076. When was Democratic People's Republic of Korea established?
September 9th, 1948

1077. What is the area of North Korea?
46,528 sq mi / 120,538 km^2

1078. How long is the coastline of North Korea?
   1,550 mi / 2,495 km
1079. What is the population of North Korea?
   24,720,407 (by 2013)
1080. What is the currency of North Korea?
   North Korean Won
1081. What is the geographical feature of the terrain of North Korea?
   Mostly hills and mountains separated by deep, narrow valleys; coastal plains wide in west, discontinuous in east
1082. What is the highest point of North Korea, located on the border between China and North Korea?
   Paektu-san (also called Baekdu Mountain, Changbai Mountain, volcanic, 9,003 ft / 2,744 m)
1083. Which crater lake lies within a caldera atop the Paektu-san?
   Heaven Lake (3.8 sq mi / 9.8 km^2)
1084. What is the lowest point of North Korea?
   Sea of Japan (0 ft / 0 m)
1085. Which highland varies between 3,281 ft (1,000 m) and 6,562 ft (2,000 m) of altitude and is the largest tableland on Korean Peninsula?
   Gamma Plateau (also called Kaema Plateau)
1086. Which mountain range stretches from north to south in central North Korea, west of the Gamma Plateau?
   Rangrim Mountains
1087. Which mountain, located in Taebaek Range, is famous for its scenic beauty?
   Geumgangsan (also called Mt Kumgang, Diamond Mountain, 5,374 ft / 1,638 m)
1088. How high is Kangnam Mountains, a mountain range in northern North Korea?
   3,432 ft / 1,046 m
1089. What is the longest river in North Korea, located on the border between North Korea and China?
   Amnok River (also called Yalu River, 491 mi / 790 km)
1090. What is the second longest river in North Korea, located on the border between North Korea, China, and Russia?
   Duman River (324 mi / 521 km)
1091. What is the third longest river in North Korea?
   Taedong River (280 mi / 450 km)
1092. Which national parks are located in North Korea?
   Songnisan National Park, Kayasan National Park, Dadohae Haesang National Park, Hallyeo Waterway National Park, and Seoraksan National Park
1093. Which national park, located in southwestern North Korea, is a marine park with about 1700 islands?
   Dadohae Haesang National Park
1094. What are administrative divisions called in North Korea?
   Provinces
1095. How many provinces does North Korea have?
   9 (plus 2 municipalities)
1096. What is the climate of North Korea?

Temperate with rainfall concentrated in summer

1097. What are the natural resources of North Korea?
Coal, lead, tungsten, zinc, graphite, magnesite, iron ore, copper, gold, pyrites, salt, fluorspar, and hydropower

1098. What are the natural hazards of North Korea?
Late spring droughts often followed by severe flooding; occasional typhoons during the early fall

1099. What are the religions of North Korea?
Traditionally Buddhist and Confucianist, some Christian and syncretic Chondogyo (Religion of the Heavenly Way)

1100. What are the ethnic groups of North Korea?
Mostly Korean; a small Chinese community and a few ethnic Japanese

Korea, South

1101. What is the official name of South Korea?
Republic of Korea

1102. Which country borders South Korea to the north?
North Korea

1103. Japan is at which direction of South Korea?
East

1104. China is at which direction of South Korea?
West

1105. Which body of water lies to the west of South Korea?
Yellow Sea
1106. Which body of water lies to the east of South Korea?
Sea of Japan
1107. Which body of water lies to the south of South Korea?
East China Sea
1108. About how many islands are there in South Korea?
3000
1109. What is the national anthem of South Korea?
The Patriotic Song
1110. What is the capital of South Korea?
Seoul (the largest city)
1111. What is the official language of South Korea?
Korean
1112. What type of government does South Korea have?
Presidential Republic
1113. When was Republic of Korea established?
August 15th, 1948
1114. What is the area of South Korea?
38,492 sq mi / 99,720 km^2
1115. How long is the coastline of South Korea?
1,499 mi / 2,413 km
1116. What is the population of South Korea?
48,955,203 (by 2013)
1117. What is the currency of South Korea?
South Korean Won
1118. What is the geographical feature of the terrain of South Korea?
Mostly hills and mountains; wide coastal plains in west and south
1119. What is the highest point of South Korea?
Hallasan (6,398 ft / 1,950 m)
1120. Halla-san is a shield volcano on which island?
Jeju-do
1121. What are three main mountains of South Korea?
Hallasan, Jirisan (6,283 ft / 1,915 m), and Seoraksan (5,603 ft / 1,708 m)
1122. What is the lowest point of South Korea?
Sea of Japan (0 ft / 0 m)
1123. What is the largest island in South Korea?
Jeju-do (712 sq mi / 1,845 km²)
1124. What are the Liancourt Rocks (also called Dokdo, Tokto, or Takeshima)?
It is a group of small islets in Sea of Japan, which is disputed between Japan and South Korea, and is administered by South Korea
1125. Which island is in the estuary of the Han River, on the west coast of South Korea?
Ganghwa Island (117 sq mi / 302 km^2)
1126. What is the longest river in South Korea?
Nakdong River (also called Rakdong, 326 mi / 525 km)

1127. What is the second longest river in South Korea?

Han River (319 mi / 514 km)

1128. What are the terrestrial national parks located in South Korea?

Jirisan National Park, Gyeongju National Park, Gyeryongsan National Park, Seoraksan National Park, Songnisan National Park, Hallasan National Park, Naejangsan National Park, Gayasan National Park, Deogyusan National Park, Odaesan National Park, Juwangsan National Park, Bukhansan National Park, Chiaksan National Park, Woraksan National Park, Sobaeksan National Park, Wolchulsan National Park, and Byeonsanban-do National Park

1129. What is the first national park and the largest terrestrial national park in South Korea?

Jirisan National Park (182 sq mi / 472 km^2)

1130. What are marine national parks located in South Korea?

Dadohae Haesang National Park, Hallyeo Haesang National Park, and Taean-haean National Park

1131. What is the largest marine national park in South Korea?

Dadohae Haesang National Park (896 sq mi / 2,322 km², water: 767 sq mi / 1,987 km²)

1132. What are administrative divisions called in South Korea?

Provinces

1133. How many provinces does South Korea have?

9 (plus 7 metropolitan cities)

1134. What is the climate of South Korea?

Temperate, with rainfall heavier in summer than winter

1135. What are the natural resources of South Korea?

Coal, tungsten, graphite, molybdenum, lead, and hydropower potential

1136. What are the natural hazards of South Korea?

Occasional typhoons bring high winds and floods; low-level seismic activity common in southwest

1137. What are the religions of South Korea?

Christian 26.3% (Protestant 19.7%, Roman Catholic 6.6%), Buddhist 23.2%, other or unknown 1.3%, none 49.3%

1138. What are the ethnic groups of South Korea?

Mostly Korean; a small Chinese community

Kuwait

1139. What is the official name of Kuwait?

State of Kuwait

1140. Which country borders Kuwait to the south?

Saudi Arabia

1141. Which country borders Kuwait to the north and northwestern?

Iraq

1142. Which body of water lies to the east of Kuwait?

Persian Gulf

1143. How many Kuwait islands are there in Persian Gulf?

9 (Warbah Island, Bubiyan Island, Miskan Island, Failaka Island, Auhah Island, Umm an Namil Island, Kubbar Island, Qaruh Island, and Umm al Maradim Island)

1144. What is the largest island in the Kuwait?
Bubiyan Island (333 sq mi / 863 km^2)

1145. Which island is believed to be the outermost point of the ancient civilization of Dilmun?
Failaka Island (7.8 sq mi / 20 km^2)

1146. Which island in Kuwait is inhibited?
Failaka Island

1147. What is the national anthem of Kuwait?
Al-Nasheed Al-Watani

1148. What is the capital of Kuwait?
Kuwait City (the largest city)

1149. What is the official language of Kuwait?
Arabic

1150. What type of government does Kuwait have?
Constitutional Emirate

1151. In 1534, Kuwait was part of which empire?
Ottoman Empire

1152. During which period did Persia occupy Kuwait?
1623 – 1638

1153. When did Kuwait become a British protectorate?
November 3rd, 1914

1154. When did Kuwait gain independence from the United Kingdom?
June 19th, 1961

1155. When was Kuwait attacked and overrun by Iraq?
August 2nd, 1990

1156. When did the United States-led United Nation coalition liberate Kuwait from Iraq?
February 28th, 1991

1157. What is the area of Kuwait?
6,878 sq mi / 17,818 km^2

1158. How long is the coastline of Kuwait?
310 mi / 499 km

1159. What is the population of Kuwait?
2,695,316 (by 2013)

1160. What is the currency of Kuwait?
Kuwaiti Dinar

1161. What is the geographical feature of the terrain of Kuwait?
Flat to slightly undulating desert plain

1162. What is the highest point of Kuwait?
Unnamed location (1,004 ft / 306 m)

1163. What is the lowest point of Kuwait?
Persian Gulf (0 ft / 0 m)

1164. How large is Jal Az-Zor National Park in Kuwait, which includes part of the cliffs of Jal Az-Zor ridge and escarpment as well as a coastal area with sand dunes, salt marshes and mud flats?
97 sq mi / 250 km^2

1165. What are administrative divisions called in Kuwait?
Governorates

1166. How many governorates does Kuwait have?
6

1167. What is the climate of Kuwait?
Dry desert; intensely hot summers; short, cool winters

1168. What are the natural resources of Kuwait?
Petroleum, fish, shrimp, and natural gas

1169. What are the natural hazards of Kuwait?
Sudden cloudbursts are common from October to April and bring heavy rain, which can damage roads and houses; sandstorms and dust storms occur throughout the year but are most common between March and August

1170. What are the religions of Kuwait?
Muslim 85% (Sunni 70%, Shia 30%), other (includes Christian, Hindu, Parsi) 15%

1171. What are the ethnic groups of Kuwait?
Kuwaiti 45%, other Arab 35%, South Asian 9%, Iranian 4%, other 7%

Kyrgyzstan

1172. What is the official name of Kyrgyzstan?
Kyrgyz Republic

1173. Which country borders Kyrgyzstan to the north?
Kazakhstan

1174. Which country borders Kyrgyzstan to the south and southwest?
Tajikistan

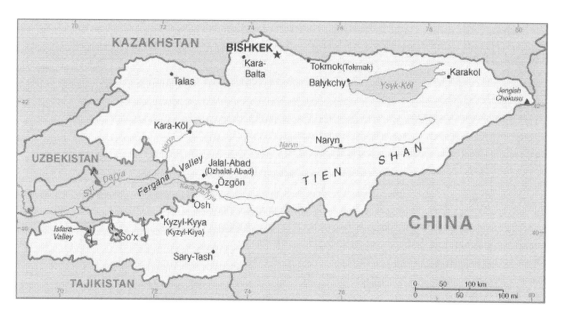

1175. Which country borders Kyrgyzstan to the west?
Uzbekistan
1176. Which country borders Kyrgyzstan to the east and southeast?
China
1177. How many enclaves of Kyrgyzstan are there, located in Uzbekistan and Tajikistan?
3
1178. What is the national anthem of Kyrgyzstan?
National Anthem of the Kyrgyz Republic
1179. What is the capital of Kyrgyzstan?
Bishkek (the largest city)
1180. What is the official language of Kyrgyzstan?
Kyrgyz and Russian
1181. What type of government does Kyrgyzstan have?
Parliamentary Republic
1182. When was Kyrgyzstan annexed by China?
March 1756

1183. When was Kyrgyzstan annexed by Russia?
February 19th, 1876

1184. When did Kyrgyzstan become the Kirghiz Soviet Socialist Republic?
December 5th, 1936

1185. When did Kyrgyzstan gain independence from the Soviet Union?
August 31st, 1991

1186. What was the 2010 Kyrgyzstan crisis?
It began in April 2010 with the ousting of Kyrgyz president Kurmanbek Bakiyev, and was followed by increased ethnic tension involving the Kyrgyz and Uzbeks in the south of the country, which escalated in June 2010

1187. What is the area of Kyrgyzstan?
77,181 sq mi / 199,951 km^2

1188. How long is the coastline of Kyrgyzstan?
0 mi / 0 km (landlocked)

1189. What is the population of Kyrgyzstan?
5,548,042 (by 2013)

1190. What is the currency of Kyrgyzstan?
Som

1191. What is the geographical feature of the terrain of Kyrgyzstan?
Peaks of Tien Shan and associated valleys and basins encompass entire nation

1192. What is the highest point of Kyrgyzstan?
Jengish Chokusu (also called Pik Pobedy, 24,406 ft / 7,439 m)

1193. Jengish Chokusu is located in which mountain range?
Tian Shan

1194. Tian Shan mountain range covers which countries?
China, Pakistan, India, Kazakhstan, Kyrgyzstan, and Uzbekistan

1195. What is the lowest point of Kyrgyzstan?
Kara-Daryya (also called Karadar'ya or Kara Darya, 433 ft / 132 m, length: 110 mi / 177 km)

1196. About how many rivers and streams in Kyrgyzstan?
40,000

1197. What is the longest river in Kyrgyzstan, located in Kyrgyzstan and Uzbekistan?
Naryn River (383 mi / 616 km, Kyrgyzstan: 332 mi / 535 km)

1198. What is the second longest river in Kyrgyzstan, located in Kyrgyzstan and Kazakhstan?
Talas River (183 mi / 294 km)

1199. What is the third longest river in Kyrgyzstan, located in Kyrgyzstan and Kazakhstan?
Chui River (137 mi / 221 km)

1200. About how many lakes are there in Kyrgyzstan?
2000

1201. What is the largest lake in Kyrgyzstan?
Issyk Kul (also called Ysyk Kol or Issyk-Kol, 2,408 sq mi / 6,236 km^2)

1202. What is Issyk Kul's rank by size among mountain lakes in the world?
2nd

1203. What are primary inflows of Issyk Kul, located in Tian Shan mountain range?
Glaciers

1204. What is the second largest lake in Kyrgyzstan?

Son Kul (104 sq mi / 270 km^2)
1205. What is the third largest lake in Kyrgyzstan?
Chatyr Kul (59 sq mi / 154 km^2)
1206. Kyrgyzstan has the world's largest natural-growth walnut forest. What is the name of the forest?
Arslanbob
1207. Which national park is an alpine national park, located in Tian Shan mountain range?
Ala Archa National Park (75 sq mi / 194 km^2)
1208. What are administrative divisions called in Kyrgyzstan?
Provinces
1209. How many provinces does Kyrgyzstan have?
7 (plus 1 city)
1210. What is the climate of Kyrgyzstan?
Dry continental to polar in high Tien Shan Mountains; subtropical in southwest (Fergana Valley); temperate in northern foothill zone
1211. What are the natural resources of Kyrgyzstan?
Abundant hydropower; significant deposits of gold and rare earth metals; locally exploitable coal, oil, and natural gas; other deposits of nepheline, mercury, bismuth, lead, and zinc
1212. What are the religions of Kyrgyzstan?
Kyrgyz 64.9%, Uzbek 13.8%, Russian 12.5%, Dungan 1.1%, Ukrainian 1%, Uyghur 1%, other 5.7%
1213. What are the ethnic groups of Kyrgyzstan?
Kyrgyz 64.9%, Uzbek 13.8%, Russian 12.5%, Dungan 1.1%, Ukrainian 1%, Uyghur 1%, other 5.7%

Laos

1214. What is the official name of Laos?
Lao People's Democratic Republic
1215. Which countries border Laos to the northwest?
Burma and China
1216. Which country borders Laos to the east?
Vietnam
1217. Which country borders Laos to the south?
Cambodia
1218. Which country borders Laos to the southwest?
Thailand
1219. What is the motto of Laos?
Peace, Independence, Democracy, Unity and Prosperity
1220. What is the national anthem of Laos?
Pheng Xat Lao
1221. What is the capital of Laos?
Vientiane (the largest city)

1222. What is the official language of Laos?

Lao

1223. What type of government does Laos have?

Socialist Republic, Communist Single-party State

1224. During which period did Lao kingdom of Lan Xang exist?

1354 – 1707

1225. When did Laos become a French protectorate as part of French Indochina?

October 3rd, 1893

1226. During which period was Laos occupied by Japan?

March 9th, 1945 – August 27th, 1945

1227. When was France protectorate re-established after World War II?

April 23rd, 1946

1228. When did Laos gain independence from France?

July 19th, 1949

1229. When did Laos become communist controlled Lao People's Democratic Republic?

December 2nd, 1975

1230. What is the area of Laos?

91,405 sq mi / 236,800 km^2

1231. How long is the coastline of Laos?

0 mi / 0 km (landlocked)

1232. What is the population of Laos?

6,695,166 (by 2013)

1233. What is the currency of Laos?

Kip

1234. What is the geographical feature of the terrain of Laos?

Mostly rugged mountains; some plains and plateaus

1235. What is the highest point of Laos?
Phu Bia (9,242 ft / 2,817 m)

1236. Phu Bia is located in which mountain range?
Annamese Cordillera

1237. What is the lowest point of Laos?
Mekong River (230 ft / 70 m)

1238. What is the longest river in Laos, located in China, Burma, Laos, Thailand, Cambodia, and Vietnam?
Mekong River (2,600 mi / 4,184 km)

1239. What are Pak Ou Caves famous for?
Lao style Buddha sculptures assembled over the centuries by local people and pilgrims

1240. Pak Ou Caves is located at the confluence of the Mekong River and which river?
Nam Ou (278 mi / 448 km)

1241. About how many Buddhas are there in Tham Ting (lower cave)?
2,500

1242. About how many Buddhas are there in Tham Theung (upper cave)?
1,500

1243. What are nation protected areas in Laos?
Nam Ha National Protected Area and Xe Pian National Protected Area

1244. What are administrative divisions called in Laos?
Provinces

1245. How many provinces does Laos have?
16

1246. What is the climate of Laos?
Tropical monsoon; rainy season (May to November); dry season (December to April)

1247. What are the natural resources of Laos?
Timber, hydropower, gypsum, tin, gold, and gemstones

1248. What are the natural hazards of Laos?
Floods, droughts

1249. What are the religions of Laos?
Buddhist 67%, Christian 1.5%, other and unspecified 31.5%

1250. What are the ethnic groups of Laos?
Lao 55%, Khmou 11%, Hmong 8%, other (over 100 minor ethnic groups) 26%

Lebanon

1251. What is the official name of Lebanon?
Lebanese Republic

1252. Which country borders Lebanon to the south?
Israel

1253. Which country borders Lebanon to the north and east?
Syria

1254. Which body of water lies to the east of Lebanon?
Mediterranean Sea

1255. What is the national anthem of Lebanon?
Lebanese National Anthem

1256. What is the capital of Lebanon?
Beirut (the largest city)

1257. What is the official language of Lebanon?
Arabic

1258. What type of government does Lebanon have?
Confessionalist, Parliamentary Republic

1259. Location of Phoenician cities of Byblos (Jubayl), Tyre, Sidon, and Beyryt (Beirut) had been ruled by which intruders during 1800 BCE – 332 BCE?
Babylonians, Persians, Greeks, Romans, Byzantines, Crusaders, and Arabs

1260. Lebanon was ruled by which empire during 1585 – 1590?
Ottoman

1261. When was Lebanon annexed by Egypt?
May 27th, 1832

1262. When was Ottoman rule restored?
October 10th, 1840

1263. When did Lebanon become the League of Nations Mandate under France administration?
September 1st, 1920

1264. When did Lebanon gain independence from the League of Nations mandate under French administration?
November 22nd, 1943

1265. Which country occupied 13 villages in Lebanon during October 30th, 1948 – March 23rd, 1949?

Israel

1266. What was the 1958 Lebanon crisis?

It was a Lebanese political crisis caused by political (pro-western and Arab nationalism) and religious tensions (Maronite Christians and Muslims) in the country; with a United States military intervention, the crisis was eased

1267. What was the Lebanese Civil War during April 13th, 1975 – October 13th, 1990?

It was a multifaceted civil war in Lebanon; The involvement of Syria, Israel, the United States and Palestine Liberation Organization (PLO) exacerbated the conflict; 130,000–250,000 people killed; Syrian occupation of Lebanon; Israeli occupation of the Southern region of Lebanon which lasted until May 22nd, 2000

1268. What was the Cedar Revolution in Lebanon?

It was a chain of demonstrations in Lebanon triggered by the assassination of the former Lebanese Prime Minister Rafik Hariri on February 14th, 2005; Syrian troops completely withdrew from Lebanon on April 27th, 2005; the Pro-Syrian government was also disbanded

1269. What was the 2006 Lebanon War (also called 2006 Israel-Hezbollah War, July War or Second Lebanon War)?

Hizballah kidnapped two Israeli soldiers leading to a 34-day military conflict between Lebanon and Israel; 1,200 Lebanese civilians were killed; Lebanese Armed Forces (LAF) deployed throughout the country for the first time in decades; both sides claimed victory

1270. What is the area of Lebanon?

4,014 sq mi / 10,400 km^2

1271. How long is the coastline of Lebanon?

140 mi / 225 km

1272. What is the population of Lebanon?

4,131,583 (by 2013)

1273. What is the currency of Lebanon?

Lebanese Pound

1274. What is the geographical feature of the terrain of Lebanon?

Narrow coastal plain; El Beqaa (Bekaa Valley) separates Lebanon and Anti-Lebanon Mountains

1275. What is the highest point of Lebanon?

Qurnat as Sawda' (10,131 ft / 3,088 m)

1276. Qurnat as Sawda' is located in which mountain range?

Mount Lebanon

1277. What is the lowest point of Lebanon?

Mediterranean Sea (0 ft / 0 m)

1278. Lebanon is well watered and there are many rivers and streams. How many rivers navigable are there in the country?

0

1279. Which three river basins cover about 45 percent of Lebanon?

Orontes River, Hasbani River, and Litani River

1280. What is the longest river in Lebanon?

Litani River (106 mi / 170 km)

1281. Which river is an ancient chief river of Levant, located in Lebanon, Syria and Turkey?

Orontes River (also called Draco, Typhon or Axius)

1282. The Hasbani River is located in Lebanon and which other country?
Israel

1283. Which river is a tourist attraction in Lebanon, which is the place where the ancient god Adonis died, and the river became red with his blood?
Nahr Ibrahim

1284. What is the only permanent lake in Lebanon?
Buhayrat al Qirawn

1285. What is Jeita Grotto?
A compound two separate but interconnected karstic limestone caves spanning an overall length of 5.6 mi (9 km) in Nahr al-Kalb Valley near Jeita

1286. What is the only national park, located in Beirut, which protects a mountainous area partly covered with pine and other trees?
Benta'ael National Park (0.8 sq mi / 2 km^2)

1287. What are administrative divisions called in Lebanon?
Governorates

1288. How many governorates does Lebanon have?
6

1289. How many new governorates have been legislated but not yet implemented?
2

1290. What is the climate of Lebanon?
Mediterranean; mild to cool, wet winters with hot, dry summers; Lebanon mountains experience heavy winter snows

1291. What are the natural resources of Lebanon?
Limestone, iron ore, salt, water-surplus state in a water-deficit region, and arable land

1292. What are the natural hazards of Lebanon?
Dust storms and sandstorms

1293. What are the religions of Lebanon?
Muslim 59.7% (Shia, Sunni, Druze, Isma'ilite, Alawite or Nusayri), Christian 39% (Maronite Catholic, Greek Orthodox, Melkite Catholic, Armenian Orthodox, Syrian Catholic, Armenian Catholic, Syrian Orthodox, Roman Catholic, Chaldean, Assyrian, Copt, Protestant), other 1.3%

1294. What are the ethnic groups of Lebanon?
Arab 95%, Armenian 4%, other 1%

Macau (China)

1295. What is Macau?
A special administrative region of China

1296. Macau is at which direction of mainland China?
South

1297. Macau is located in which body of water?
South China Sea

1298. Macau is at the mouth of which delta?
Pearl River Delta

1299. What are the official languages of Macau?
Chinese and Portuguese
1300. In which year did Macau become a Portugal administered trading post?
1557
1301. When did Macau become a Portuguese colony?
December 1st, 1887
1302. When did Macau become Macau Special Administrative Region of China?
December 20th, 1999
1303. What is the area of Macau?
11 sq mi / 28 km^2
1304. How long is the coastline of Macau?
25 mi / 41 km
1305. What is the population of Macau?
583,003 (by 2013)
1306. What is the geographical feature of the terrain of Macau?
Generally flat
1307. What is the highest point of Macau?
Coloane Alto (564 ft / 172 m)
1308. What is the lowest point of Macau?
South China Sea (0 ft / 0 m)
1309. Macau was once an island, how did it become a peninsula?
By land reclaim
1310. Macau is composed of Macau Peninsula and which two islands?
Taipa Island and Coloane Island

1311. What is the climate of Macau?

Subtropical; marine with cool winters, warm summers

1312. What are the natural hazards of Macau?

Typhoons

1313. What are the religions of Macau?

Buddhist 50%, Roman Catholic 15%, none or other 35%

1314. What are the ethnic groups of Macau?

Chinese 94.3%, other 5.7% (includes Macanese - mixed Portuguese and Asian ancestry)

Malaysia

1315. Which body of water separates Malaysia into two regions, Peninsular Malaysia and East Malaysia (also called Malaysian Borneo)?

South China Sea

1316. Which country borders Peninsular Malaysia to the north?

Thailand

1317. Which strait separates Malaysia from Singapore?

Strait of Johor (also called Tebrau Strait, Johor Strait, Selat Johor, Selat Tebrau, or Tebrau Reach)

1318. Which country borders East Malaysia to the south?
Indonesia

1319. Which country borders East Malaysia in the north?
Brunei

1320. East Malaysia is located on which island?
Borneo

1321. What is the largest unshared island in Malaysia?
Banggi Island (170 sq mi / 441 km²)

1322. What is the second largest unshared island in Malaysia?
Betruit Island (161 sq mi / 417 km²)

1323. What is the motto of Malaysia?
Unity Is Strength

1324. What is the national anthem of Malaysia?
My Country

1325. What is the capital of Malaysia?
Kuala Lumpur (the largest city)

1326. The seat of the federal government was shifted in 1999 to which city due to the overcrowding and congestion in Kuala Lumpur?
Putrajaya

1327. What is the official language of Malaysia?
Malay

1328. What type of government does Malaysia have?
Federal Constitutional Monarchy

1329. Malaysia state, Malacca, was colonized by which country during 1511 – 1641?
Portugul

1330. Malacca was colonized by which country during 1641 – 1824?
Netherlands

1331. During 1895 – 1946, which country colonized the Federated Malay States (Selangor, Perak, Negeri Sembilan and Pahang) and the Unfederated Malay States (Johor, Kedah, Kelantan, Perlis, and Terengganu)?
United Kingdom

1332. What are the Straits Settlements during 1826 – 1946?
A group of British territories located in present-day Malaysia (Malacca, Penang, and Labuan Island) and Singapore

1333. Malaysia was occupied by which country during January 31st, 1942 – September 12th, 1945?
Japan

1334. Why did the United Kingdom form the Malayan Union to combine the Federated Malay States, the Unfederated Malay States, and the Straits Settlements during 1946 – 1948?
To unify Malay Peninsula under a single government to simplify administration

1335. When was the Federation of Malaya established?
January 31st, 1948

1336. When did the Federation of Malaya gain independence from the United Kingdom?
August 31st, 1957

1337. When was Malaysia established?
September 16th, 1963?

1338. When did Singapore withdraw from Malaysia?
August 9th, 1965

1339. What is the area of Malaysia?
127,321 sq mi / 329,847 km^2

1340. How long is the coastline of Malaysia?
2,905 mi / 4,675 km

1341. What is the population of Malaysia?
29,628,392 (by 2013)

1342. What is the currency of Malaysia?
Ringgit

1343. What is the geographical feature of the terrain of Malaysia?
Coastal plains rising to hills and mountains

1344. What is the highest point of Malaysia, located in East Malaysia?
Mount Kinabalu (13,451 ft / 4,100 m)

1345. Mount Kinabalu is located in which mountain range?
Crocker Range

1346. What is the highest point of Peninsular Malaysia?
Mount Tahan (7,175 ft / 2,187 m)

1347. Mount Tahan is located in which mountain range?
Tahan Range

1348. What is the lowest point of Malaysia?
Indian Ocean (0 ft / 0 m)

1349. What is the longest river in Malaysia, located in East Malaysia?
Rajang River (350 mi / 563 km)

1350. What is the second longest river in Malaysia, located in East Malaysia?
Kinabatangan River (348 mi / 560 km)

1351. What is the longest river in Peninsular Malaysia?
Pahang River (285 mi / 459 km)

1352. What is the largest artificial lake in Southeast Asia, located in Peninsular Malaysia?
Kenyir Lake (100 sq mi / 260 km²)

1353. About how many small islands are there in Kenyir Lake?
340

1354. Which national parks are located in Malaysia?
Endau Rompin National Park, Gunung Ledang Johor National Park, Tanjung Piai Johor National Park, Pulau Kukup Johor National Park, Islands off Mersing Johor National Park, Taman Negara National Park, Penang National Park, Bako National Park, Gunung Mulu National Park, Niah National Park, Lambir Hills National Park, Similajau National Park, Gunung Gading National Park, Kubah National Park, Batang Ai National Park, Loagan Bunut National Park, Tanjung Datu National Park, Talang Satang National Park, Bukit Tiban National Park, Maludam National Park, Rajang Mangroves National Park, Gunung Buda National Park, Pulong Tau National Park, Kuching Wetlands National Park, and Santubong National Park

1355. What is the largest national park in Malaysia, located in Peninsular Malaysia, which includes

Mount Tahan?
Taman Negara National Park (1,676 sq mi / 4,343 km²)

1356. What is the second largest national park in Malaysia, located in Peninsular Malaysia, which is a protected tropical rainforest?
Endau Rompin National Park (336 sq mi / 870 km²)

1357. What is the largest national park in East Malaysia, which is famous for enormous caves, vast cave networks, rock pinnacles, cliffs and gorges?
Gunung Mulu National Park (291 sq mi / 754 km²)

1358. What is the largest known underground chamber in the world, located in Gunung Mulu National Park?
Sarawak Chamber (2,300 ft / 700 m long, 1,300 ft / 400 m wide, and 230 ft / 70 m high)

1359. What is the longest cave in Asia, located in Gunung Mulu National Park?
Clearwater (66 mi / 107 km)

1360. What are administrative divisions called in Malaysia?
States

1361. How many states does Malaysia have?
13 (plus 1 federal territory)

1362. What is the climate of Malaysia?
Tropical; annual southwest (April to October) and northeast (October to February) monsoons

1363. What are the natural resources of Malaysia?
Tin, petroleum, timber, copper, iron ore, natural gas, and bauxite

1364. What are the natural hazards of Malaysia?
Flooding; landslides; forest fires

1365. What are the religions of Malaysia?
Muslim 60.4%, Buddhist 19.2%, Christian 9.1%, Hindu 6.3%, Confucianism, Taoism, other traditional Chinese religions 2.6%, other or unknown 1.5%, none 0.8%

1366. What are the ethnic groups of Malaysia?
Malay 50.4%, Chinese 23.7%, indigenous 11%, Indian 7.1%, others 7.8%

Maldives

1367. What is the official name of Maldives?
Republic of Maldives

1368. Maldives is located in which body of water?
Laccadive Sea (also called Lakshadweep Sea)

1369. Sri Lanka is at which direction of Maldives?
Northeast

1370. How many atolls are there in Maldives?
26

1371. How many coral islands are there in Maldives?
1,190 (about 200 inhabited)

1372. What is the largest island in Maldives?
Gan

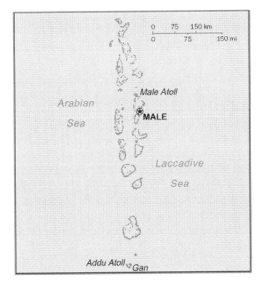

1373. What is the national anthem of Maldives?
National Salute

1374. What is the capital of Maldives?
Malé (the largest city)

1375. What is the official language of Maldives?
Dhivehi (also called Mahl)

1376. What type of government does Maldives have?
Presidential Republic

1377. Maldives was settled by Buddhists from where in 5th century?
Ceylon (the present-day Sri Lanka)

1378. Maldives was under whose protection from Ceylon in 1645?
Dutch

1379. Maldives was under whose protection from Ceylon on February 16th, 1796?
British

1380. When did Maldives become a British protectorate?
December 16th, 1887

1381. During which period southern atolls were succeeded as the United Suvadive Republic?
January 3rd, 1959 – September 30th, 1963

1382. When did Maldives gain independence from the United Kingdom?
July 26th, 1965

1383. When did Maldivians abolish the sultanate and establish a republic?
November 11th, 1968

1384. What is the area of Maldives?
115 sq mi / 298 km^2

1385. What is Maldives' rank by size in Asia?
Smallest

1386. How long is the coastline of Maldives?
400 mi / 644 km

1387. What is the population of Maldives?

393,988 (by 2013)
1388. What is Maldives' rank by population in Asia?
Least
1389. What is the currency of Maldives?
Maldivian Rufiyaa
1390. What is the geographical feature of the terrain of Maldives?
Flat, with white sandy beaches
1391. What is the highest point of Maldives?
Unnamed location on Wilingili Island in the Addu Atoll (7.9 ft / 2.4 m)
1392. What is Maldives' rank by the highest point in world?
Lowest
1393. What is Maldives' rank by the average height in the world?
Lowest (4.9 ft / 1.5 m)
1394. What is the lowest point of Maldives?
Indian Ocean (0 ft / 0 m)
1395. What are administrative divisions called in Maldives?
Atolls
1396. How many districts does Maldives have?
19
1397. What is the climate of Maldives?
Tropical; hot, humid; dry, northeast monsoon (November to March); rainy, southwest monsoon (June to August)
1398. What are the natural resources of Maldives?
Fish
1399. What are the natural hazards of Maldives?
Tsunamis; low elevation of islands makes them sensitive to sea level rise
1400. What are the religions of Maldives?
Sunni Muslim
1401. What are the ethnic groups of Maldives?
South Indians, Sinhalese, Arabs

Mongolia

1402. Which country borders Mongolia to the north?
Russia
1403. Which country borders Mongolia to the south, east and west?
China
1404. What is the national anthem of Mongolia?
National anthem of Mongolia
1405. What is the capital of Mongolia?
Ulaanbaatar (the largest city)
1406. What is the official language of Mongolia?
Mongolian
1407. What type of government does Mongolia have?
Parliamentary Republic

1408. Which nomadic empires ruled Mongolia?
Xiongnu, Xianbei, Rouran, and Gokturks

1409. Who became the ruler of all Mongols in 1206?
Genghis Khan

1410. About how large was the Mongol Empire during 1206 – 1368?
9,266,000 sq mi / 24,000,000 km^2 (the largest contiguous empire in the history of the world; Stretching from Danube to Sea of Japan and from northern Siberia to Camboja; 22% of the Earth's total land area; Over 100 million people)

1411. In which year did Mongolia adopt the Tibetan Buddhism?
1577

1412. When was Mongolia ruled by China and called "Outer Mongolia"?
May 1691

1413. When did Mongolia gain independence from China for the first time?
December 1st, 1911

1414. During which period was Mongolia a Russian protectorate?
November 3rd, 1912 – November 8th, 1917

1415. When was Mongolia re-annexed by China?
February 19th, 1920

1416. When did Mongolia regain independence from China?
    July 11th, 1921
1416. When did Mongolia regain independence from China?
    July 11th, 1921
1417. What is the area of Mongolia?
    630,749 sq mi / 1,564,116 km^2
1418. How long is the coastline of Mongolia?
    0 mi / 0 km (landlocked)
1419. What is Mongolia's rank by size among landlocked countries in the world?
    2nd
1420. What is the population of Mongolia?
    3,226,516 (by 2013)
1421. What is the currency of Mongolia?
    Togrog
1422. What is the geographical feature of the terrain of Mongolia?
    Vast semi-desert and desert plains, grassy steppe, mountains in west and southwest; Gobi Desert in south-central
1423. What is the highest point of Mongolia?
    Nayramadlin Orgil (also called Huyten Orgil, Khuiten Peak, or Friendship Peak, 14,350 ft / 4,374 m)
1424. Nayramadlin Orgil is the second highest point of which mountain range?
    Altai Mountains
1425. What is the lowest point of Mongolia?
    Hoh Nuur (1,699 ft / 518 m)
1426. What is the largest lake by size in Mongolia?
    Uvs Nuur (also called Lake Uvs or Uvs Lake, 1,290 sq mi / 3,350 km^2)
1427. What is the largest lake by volume in Mongolia?
    Khovsgol Nuur (freshwater, 91 cu mi / 381 km^3)
1428. What is Khovsgol Nuur's rank by size among lakes in Mongolia?
    2nd (1,065 sq mi / 2,760 km^2)
1429. What is the large semi-arid depression in Mongolia, which is bounded by the Altai Mountains by the west, Khangai Mountains by the east, and Tannu-Ola Mountains in Russian by the north?
    Great Lakes Depression (about 38,600 sq mi / 100,000 km^2)
1430. What are six major Mongolian lakes located in Great Lakes Depression?
    Uvs Nuur (saline), Khar-Us Nuur (freshwater), Khyargas Nuur (saline), Khar Nuur (freshwater), Airag Nuur (freshwater), and Dorgon Nuur (saline)
1431. What is the large desert in Mongolia, located in Mongolia and China?
    Gobi Desert
1432. About how many rivers are there in Mongolia?
    4000
1433. Which major rivers have their headwaters in Mongolia's mountain ranges?
    Yenisei, Lena and Amur
1434. What is the longest river in Mongolia?
    Orkhon River (698 mi /1,124 km)
1435. The Orkhon River is a tributary of which river, located in Mongolia and Russia?
    Selenge River (616 mi / 992 km)

1436. Which national parks are located in Mongolia?
Altai Tavan Bogd National Park, Gobi Gurvansaikhan National Park, Gorkhi-Terelj National Park, Gorkhi-Terelj National Park, Khustain Nuruu National Park, Lake Khovsgol National Park, Khar Us Nuur National Park, Onon-Balj National Park, Khan Khukhii-Khyargas Nuur National Park, and Tsambagarav National Park

1437. What is the largest national park in Mongolia, which is named after Gurvan Saikhan Mountains located in southern Mongolia?
Gobi Gurvansaikhan National Park (10,422 sq mi / 27,000 km²)

1438. What is the second largest national park in Mongolia, located in western Mongolia?
Khar Us Nuur National Park (3,282 sq mi / 8,503 km²)

1439. What is the third largest national park in Mongolia, which includes the lake with largest volume of Khovsgol Nuur?
Lake Khovsgol National Park (3,235 sq mi / 8,381 km²)

1440. What are administrative divisions called in Mongolia?
Provinces

1441. How many provinces does Mongolia have?
21

1442. What is the climate of Mongolia?
Desert; continental (large daily and seasonal temperature ranges)

1443. What are the natural resources of Mongolia?
Oil, coal, copper, molybdenum, tungsten, phosphates, tin, nickel, zinc, fluorspar, gold, silver, and iron

1444. What are the natural hazards of Mongolia?
Dust storms; grassland and forest fires; drought; "zud," which is harsh winter conditions

1445. What are the religions of Mongolia?
Buddhist Lamaist 50%, Shamanist and Christian 6%, Muslim 4%, none 40%

1446. What are the ethnic groups of Mongolia?
Mongol (mostly Khalkha) 94.9%, Turkic (mostly Kazakh) 5%, other (including Chinese and Russian) 0.1%

Nepal

1447. What is the official name of Nepal?
Federal Democratic Republic of Nepal

1448. Which country borders Nepal to the north?
China

1449. Which country borders Nepal to the south, east, and west?
India

1450. What is the motto of Nepal?
Mother and Motherland are Greater than Heaven

1451. What is the national anthem of Nepal?
We are Hundreds of Flowers

1452. What is the capital of Nepal?
Kathmandu (the largest city)

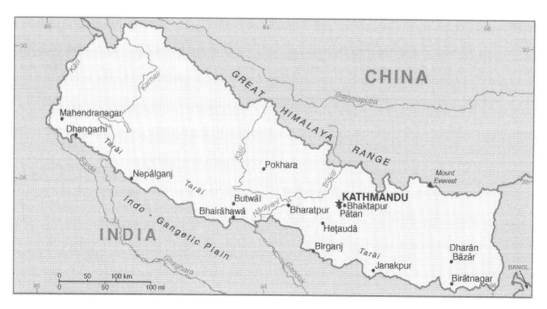

1453. What is the official language of Nepal?
Nepali

1454. What type of government does Nepal have?
Federal Democratic Republic

1455. When was the Kingdom of Nepal (also called Gorkhali Kingdom) established?
December 21th, 1768

1456. What was the Gurkha War (also called Gorkha War or Anglo-Nepalese War) during 1814 – 1816?
It was a war fought between Nepal and the British East India Company as a result of border tensions and ambitious expansionism; Treaty of Sugauli was signed in 1816, which ceded around a third of Nepal's territory to the British

1457. What is Greater Nepal?
It is a concept referring to Nepal's territories before Treaty of Sugauli, which includes some areas in India

1458. What was the Nepali Civil War during February 13th, 1996 – November 21st, 2006?
It was a conflict between government forces and Maoist rebels in Nepal, who aimed to overthrow Nepalese monarchy and establish "People's Republic of Nepal"; a Maoist victory;

Abolition of the Monarchy

1459. What was the Nepalese royal massacre that occurred on June 1st, 2001?
Crown Prince Dipendra went on a shooting-spree, assassinating 9 members of the royal family, including King Birendra and Queen Aishwarya, before shooting himself

1460. Nepal was governed by what type of government from January 15th, 2007?
A unicameral legislature under an interim constitution

1461. When was the Kingdom of Nepal abolished and the Federal Democratic Republic of Nepal established?
May 28th, 2008

1462. What is the area of Nepal?
56,812 sq mi / 147,181 km^2

1463. How long is the coastline of Nepal?
0 mi / 0 km (landlocked)

1464. What is the population of Nepal?
30,430,267 (by 2013)

1465. What is the currency of Nepal?
Rupee

1466. What is the geographical feature of the terrain of Nepal?
Tarai or flat river plain of the Ganges in south, central hill region, rugged Himalayas in north

1467. What is the highest point of Nepal?
Mount Everest (29,035 ft / 8,850 m)

1468. Mount Everest is located in which mountain range?
Himalayas

1469. How many glaciers are there in Nepal?
3,252

1470. What is the lowest point of Nepal?
Kanchan Kalan (230 ft / 70 m)

1471. Why is the Kathmandu Valley culturally important?
It lies at the crossroads of ancient civilizations of Asia, and has at least 130 important monuments, including several places of pilgrimage for Hindus and Buddhists; there are seven UNESCO World Heritage Sites within this valley

1472. What are three major rivers in Nepal?
Gandaki River, Kosi River, and Ghaghara River

1473. What is the longest river in Nepal, located in China, Nepal, and India?
Ghaghara River (also called Karnali River, 671 mi / 1,080 km)

1474. How long is the Kosi River (also called Koshi River or Saptakoshi River), located in Nepal and India?
453 mi / 729 km

1475. How long is the Gandaki River (also called Kali Gandaki, Narayani River, or Gandak River), located in China, Nepal, and India?
391 mi / 630 km

1476. The Ghaghara River, Kosi River, and Gandaki River are tributaries of which river?
Ganges River

1477. What is the largest lake in Nepal?
Rara Lake (3.9 sq mi / 10 km^2)

1478. What is the deepest lake in Nepal?
Phoksundo Lake (476 ft / 145 m)
1479. What national parks are there in Nepal?
Banke National Park, Bardia National Park, Chitwan National Park, Khaptad National Park, Langtang National Park, Makalu Barun National Park , Rara National Park, Sagarmatha National Park, Shey Phoksundo National Park, and Shivapuri Nagarjun National Park
1480. What is the largest national park in Nepal, which includes Phoksundo Lake?
Shey Phoksundo National Park (1,372 sq mi / 3,555 km^2)
1481. What is the second largest national park in Nepal, located in Himalayas, which is the world's only protected area with an elevation of more than 26,000 ft (8,000 m) including tropical forest as well as snow-capped peaks?
Makalu Barun National Park (899 sq mi / 2,330 km²)
1482. What is the third largest national park in Nepal, located in Himalayas, which includes the sacred Gosainkunda Lake?
Langtang National Park (660 sq mi / 1,710 km^2)
1483. What is the fourth largest national park in Nepal, located in Himalayas, which includes the southern half of Mount Everest?
Sagarmatha National Park (443 sq mi / 1,148 km^2)
1484. Rara Lake is located in which national park?
Rara National Park (41 sq mi / 106 km^2)
1485. Bardia National Park (374 sq mi / 968 km^2) and Banke National Park (212 sq mi / 550 km²) represent the biggest conservation area in Asia of what kind?
Tiger Conservation
1486. What are administrative divisions called in Nepal?
Zones
1487. How many zones does Nepal have?
14
1488. What is the climate of Nepal?
Varies from cool summers and severe winters in north to subtropical summers and mild winters in south
1489. What are the natural resources of Nepal?
Quartz, water, timber, hydropower, scenic beauty, small deposits of lignite, copper, cobalt, and iron ore
1490. What are the natural hazards of Nepal?
Severe thunderstorms; flooding; landslides; drought and famine depending on the timing, intensity, and duration of the summer monsoons
1491. What are the religions of Nepal?
Hindu 80.6%, Buddhist 10.7%, Muslim 4.2%, Kirant 3.6%, other 0.9%
1492. What are the ethnic groups of Nepal?
Chhettri 15.5%, Brahman-Hill 12.5%, Magar 7%, Tharu 6.6%, Tamang 5.5%, Newar 5.4%, Muslim 4.2%, Kami 3.9%, Yadav 3.9%, other 32.7%, unspecified 2.8%

Oman

1493. What is the official name of Oman?
      Sultanate of Oman
1494. Which country borders Oman to the northwest?
      United Arab Emirates
1495. Which country borders Oman to the southwest?
      Yemen
1496. Which country borders Oman to the west?
      Saudi Arabia
1497. Which body of water lies to the northeast of Oman?
      Gulf of Oman
1498. Which body of water lies to the southeast of Oman?
      Arabian Sea
1499. Oman contains which two exclaves on the Gulf of Oman, and surrounded by United Arab
      Emirates on the land side?
      Madha (29 sq mi / 75 km^2) and Musandam (695 sq mi / 1,800 km^2)
1500. Which exclave of United Arab Emirates is located inside Madha?
      Nahwa (5 mi / 8 km long)
1501. Musandam peninsula juts into which strait, which is a narrow, strategically important
      waterway between Gulf of Oman and Persian Gulf?
      Strait of Hormuz
1502. What is the national anthem of Oman?
      National Anthem of Oman
1503. What is the capital of Oman?
      Muscat (the largest city)

1504. What is the official language of Oman?
Arabic

1505. What type of government does Oman have?
Islamic Absolute Monarchy

1506. During which century did Oman adopt Islam?
7th

1507. Muscat was occupied by whom during April 1st, 1515 – January 26th, 1650
Portuguese

1508. Muscat was occupied by whom during 1550 – 1551 and 1581 – 1588?
Ottomans

1509. Muscat was occupied by whom during 1741 - 1749?
Persia

1510. In which year, Qaboos bin Said Al-Said overthrew his father, and has ruled as sultan ever since?
1970

1511. What was the Dhofar Rebellion during 1962–1975?
It was a rebellion launched in Dhofar Region against the Sultanate of Muscat and Oman as well as the United Kingdom from 1962 to 1975; the rebels were defeated, but Oman was radically reformed and modernized

1512. What is the area of Oman?
119,467 sq mi / 309,500 km^2

1513. How long is the coastline of Oman?
1,300 mi / 2,092 km

1514. What is the population of Oman?
3,154,134 (by 2013)

1515. What is the currency of Oman?
Rial

1516. What is the geographical feature of the terrain of Oman?
Central desert plain, rugged mountains in north and south

1517. What is the highest point of Oman?
Jabal Shams (9,777 ft / 2,980 m)

1518. Jabal Shams is located in which mountain range, located in Oman and United Arab Emirates?
Al Hajar Mountains

1519. What is the lowest point of Oman?
Arabian Sea (0 ft / 0 m)

1520. What are administrative divisions called in Oman?
Regions

1521. How many regions does Oman have?
5 (plus 4 governorates)

1522. What is the climate of Oman?
Dry desert; hot, humid along coast; hot, dry interior; strong southwest summer monsoon (May to September) in far south

1523. What are the natural resources of Oman?
Petroleum, copper, asbestos, some marble, limestone, chromium, gypsum, and natural gas

1524. What are the natural hazards of Oman?

Summer winds often raise large sandstorms and dust storms in interior; periodic droughts

1525. What are the religions of Oman?

Ibadhi Muslim 75%, other (includes Sunni Muslim, Shia Muslim, Hindu) 25%

1526. What are the ethnic groups of Oman?

Arab, Baluchi, South Asian (Indian, Pakistani, Sri Lankan, Bangladeshi), African

Pakistan

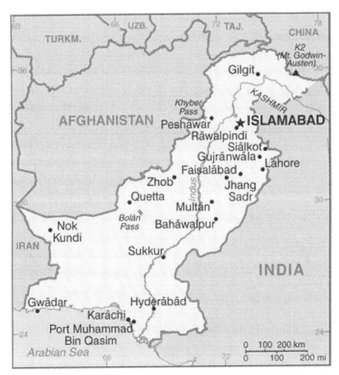

1527. What is the official name of Pakistan?

Islamic Republic of Pakistan

1528. Which country borders Pakistan to the northeast?

China

1529. Which country borders Pakistan to the east?

India

1530. Which country borders Pakistan to the northwest?

Afghanistan

1531. Which country borders Pakistan to the west?

Iran

1532. Which body of water lies to the south of Pakistan?

Arabian Sea

1533. What is the motto of Pakistan?

Unity, Discipline and Faith

1534. What is the national anthem of Pakistan?

Qaumi Tarana

1535. What is the capital of Pakistan?
Islamabad (the largest city)

1536. What is the largest city of Pakistan?
Karachi

1537. What are the official languages of Pakistan?
Urdu and English

1538. What type of government does Pakistan have?
Federal Parliamentary Republic

1539. When did Pakistan gain independence from the United Kingdom?
August 14th, 1947 (British Raj was split into Pakistan and India)

1540. What is the area of Pakistan?
340,403 sq mi / 796,095 km^2

1541. How long is the coastline of Pakistan?
650 mi / 1,046 km

1542. What is the population of Pakistan?
193,238,868 (by 2013)

1543. What is the currency of Pakistan?
Pakistani Rupee

1544. What is the geographical feature of the terrain of Pakistan?
Flat Indus plain in east; mountains in north and northwest; Balochistan plateau in west

1545. What is the highest point of Pakistan?
K2 (also called Mount Godwin-Austen, 28,251 ft / 8,611 m)

1546. K2 is located in which mountain range?
Karakoram

1547. How many peaks are above 22,966 ft (7,000 m) in Pakistan?
108

1548. What is the second highest point of Pakistan?
Nanga Parbat (26,660 ft / 8,126 m)

1549. What is the third highest point of Pakistan, located on the border of Pakistan and China?
Gasherbrum I (also called Hidden Peak or K5, 26,509 ft / 8,080 m)

1550. What is the fourth highest point of Pakistan, located on the border of Pakistan and China?
Broad Peak (also called K3, or Faichan Kangri, 26,414 ft / 8,051 m)

1551. What is the fifth highest point of Pakistan, located on the border of Pakistan and China?
Gasherbrum II (also called K4, 26,362 ft / 8,035 m)

1552. What is the lowest point of Pakistan?
Indian Ocean (0 ft / 0 m)

1553. What is the longest river in Pakistan, located in China, India, and Pakistan?
Indus River (1,976 mi / 3,180 km)

1554. What is the largest lake in Pakistan?
Lake Manchar

1555. What is the highest lake in Pakistan?
Rush Lake (15,400 ft / 4,694 m)

1556. Which two passes between Pakistan and Afghanistan were traditional migration routes between Central Eurasia and South Asia?

Khyber Pass and Bolan Pass

1557. Which national parks are located in Pakistan?
Ayubia National Park, Central Karakoram National Park, Chitral Gol National Park, Deosai National Park, Hazarganji Chiltan National Park, Hingol National Park, Khunjerab National Park, Kirthar National Park, Lal Suhanra National Park, Machiara National Park, and Margalla Hills National Park

1558. What is the largest national park in Pakistan, located in Gilgit-Baltistan Territory, which includes some of the world's highest peaks (including K2) and largest glaciers?
Central Karakoram National Park (3,860 sq mi / 10,000 km^2)

1559. What is the second largest national park in Pakistan, located in Balochistan Province, which is home to more than 35 species of mammals, 65 species of amphibians and reptiles, 185 species of birds, and 250 plant species?
Hingol National Park (2,355 sq mi / 6,100 km^2)

1560. What is the third largest national park in Pakistan, located in Gilgit-Baltistan Territory, which is at an average height of 13,500 ft (4,115 m) above sea level?
Deosai National Park (1,383 sq mi / 3,584 km^2)

1561. What are administrative divisions called in Pakistan?
Provinces

1562. How many provinces does Pakistan have?
4 (plus 1 territory and 1 capital territory)

1563. Which two territories are located in Pakistani administered portion of the disputed Jammu and Kashmir?
Azad Kashmir and Gilgit-Baltistan

1564. What is the climate of Pakistan?
Mostly hot, dry desert; temperate in northwest; arctic in north

1565. What are the natural resources of Pakistan?
Land, extensive natural gas reserves, limited petroleum, poor quality coal, iron ore, copper, salt, and limestone

1566. What are the natural hazards of Pakistan?
Frequent earthquakes, occasionally severe especially in north and west; flooding along the Indus after heavy rains (July and August)

1567. What are the religions of Pakistan?
Muslim 95% (Sunni 75%, Shia 20%), other (includes Christian and Hindu) 5%

1568. What are the ethnic groups of Pakistan?
Punjabi 44.68%, Pashtun (Pathan) 15.42%, Sindhi 14.1%, Sariaki 8.38%, Muhajirs 7.57%, Balochi 3.57%, other 6.28%

Philippines

1569. What is the official name of the Philippines?
Republic of the Philippines

1570. Taiwan is at which direction of the Philippines, across Luzon Strait?
North

1571. Vietnam is at which direction of the Philippines, across South China Sea?
West

1572. Borneo Island is at which direction of the Philippines, across Sulu Sea?
Southwest

1573. Indonesia is at which direction of the Philippines, across Celebes Sea?
South

1574. Which body of water lies to the east of the Philippines?
Philippine Sea

1575. How many islands are there in the Philippines?
7,107

1576. What are three main geographical island groups in the Philippines?
Luzon, Visayas, and Mindanao

1577. The Luzon island group includes which islands?
Luzon Island, Palawan, Mindoro, Marinduque, Masbate and Batanes Islands

1578. What are the largest islands in the Visayas island group?
Panay, Negros, Cebu, Bohol, Leyte, and Samar

1579. Mindanao island group include which islands?
Mindanao Island and Sulu Archipelago

1580. What is the largest island in the Philippines?
Luzon (40,420 sq mi / 104,688 km^2)

1581. What is the second largest island in the Philippines?
Mindanao (37,657 sq mi / 97,530 km^2)

1582. The eleven largest islands contain what percentage of the total land area of the Philippines?
94%

1583. What is the motto of the Philippines?
For God, People, Nature, and Country

1584. What is the national anthem of the Philippines?
Chosen Land

1585. What is the capital of the Philippines?
Manila

1586. Manila is located in which island?
Luzon

1587. What is the largest city of the Philippines?
Quezon City

1588. Quezon City is located in which island?
Luzon

1589. What are the official languages of the Philippines?
Filipino and English

1590. What type of government does the Philippines have?
Republic

1591. When was the Philippines discovered and claimed for Spain by Ferdinand Magellan?
March 16th, 1521

1592. During which period was the Philippines occupied by the United Kingdom?
Oct 6th, 1762 – February 10th, 1763

1593. When did the Philippines, as the First Philippine Republic, gain independence from Spain?
June 12th, 1898

1594. When did the Philippines become a United States territory following the Spanish – American War?
August 13th, 1898

1595. When did the United States abolish the First Philippine Republic?
April 16th, 1902

1596. When did the Philippines gain partial autonomy to be the Commonwealth of the Philippines?
November 15th, 1935

1597. During which period, was the Philippines occupied by Japan?
January 3rd, 1942 – August 17th, 1945

1598. When did the Philippines gain independence from the United States?
July 4th, 1946
1599. What is the area of the Philippines?
115,800 sq mi / 300,000 km^2
1600. How long is the coastline of the Philippines?
22,549 mi / 36,289 km
1601. What is the population of the Philippines?
105,720,644 (by 2013)
1602. What is the currency of the Philippines?
Peso
1603. What is the geographical feature of the terrain of the Philippines?
Mostly mountains with narrow to extensive coastal lowlands
1604. What is the highest point of Philippines?
Mount Apo (9,692 ft / 2,954 m)
1605. Mount Apo is what type of mountain?
A large solfataric, potentially active stratovolcano
1606. What is the lowest point of the Philippines?
Philippine Sea (0 ft / 0 m)
1607. What is the second highest point of the Philippines?
Mount Dulang-dulang (also called D2, 9,639 ft / 2,938 m)
1608. Mount Apo and Mount Dulang-dulang are located on which island?
Mindanao
1609. What is the third highest point of the Philippines?
Mount Pulag (9,587 ft / 2,922 m)
1610. Mount Pulag is located on which island?
Luzon
1611. Mayon Volcano is an active stratovolcano on which island?
Luzon
1612. Taal Volcano is a complex volcano on which island?
Luzon
1613. What is the longest river in the Philippines, located on Luzon?
Cagayan River (314 mi / 505 km)
1614. What is the second longest river in the Philippines, located on Mindanao?
Mindanao River (also called Rio Grande de Mindanao, 232 mi / 373 km)
1615. What is the third longest river in the Philippines, located on Mindanao?
Agusan River (217 mi / 350 km)
1616. What is the largest lake in the Philippines?
Laguna de Bay (366 sq mi / 949 km²)
1617. What is the world's second largest contiguous coral reef system and the largest in the Philippines?
Apo Reef
1618. Which national parks are located in the Philippines?
Hundred Islands National Park and Tubbataha Reef National Marine Park
1619. How large is Hundred Islands National Park, located in the northern Philippines, which are composed of ancient corals that extend well inland?

6 sq mi / 17 km²

1620. How large is Tubbataha Reef National Marine Park, located in Sulu Sea of the Philippines, which contains a reef of enormous size?
374 sq mi / 968 km²

1621. What are administrative divisions called in the Philippines?
Provinces

1622. How many provinces does the Philippines have?
80 (plus 120 chartered cities)

1623. What is the climate of the Philippines?
Tropical marine; northeast monsoon (November to April); southwest monsoon (May to October)

1624. What are the natural resources of the Philippines?
Timber, petroleum, nickel, cobalt, silver, gold, salt, and copper

1625. What are the natural hazards of the Philippines?
Astride typhoon belt, usually affected by 15 and struck by five to six cyclonic storms per year; landslides; active volcanoes; destructive earthquakes; tsunamis

1626. What are the religions of the Philippines?
Roman Catholic 80.9%, Muslim 5%, Evangelical 2.8%, Iglesia ni Kristo 2.3%, Aglipayan 2%, other Christian 4.5%, other 1.8%, unspecified 0.6%, none 0.1%

1627. What are the ethnic groups of the Philippines?
Tagalog 28.1%, Cebuano 13.1%, Ilocano 9%, Bisaya/Binisaya 7.6%, Hiligaynon Ilonggo 7.5%, Bikol 6%, Waray 3.4%, other 25.3%

Qatar

1628. What is the official name of Qatar?
State of Qatar

1629. Which country borders Qatar to the south?
Saudi Arabia

1630. Bahrain is at which direction of Qatar?
Northwest

1631. Qatar Peninsula is located in which body of water?
Persian Gulf

1632. What is the national anthem of Qatar?
National Anthem of Qatar

1633. What is the capital of Qatar?
Doha (the largest city)

1634. What is the official language of Qatar?
Arabic

1635. What type of government does Qatar have?
Emirate / Absolute Monarchy

1636. Qatar was part of which empire during 1550 – 1670?
Ottoman Empire

1637. When did Qatar become a British protectorate?
November 3rd, 1916

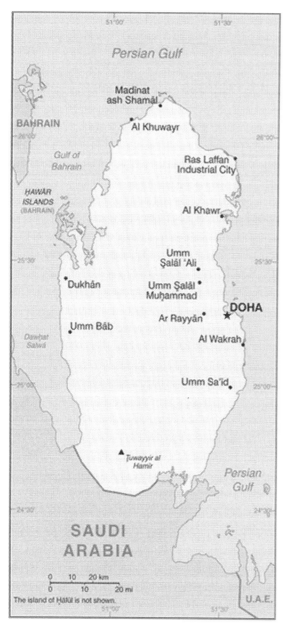

1638. When did Qatar gain independence from the United Kingdom?
    September 3rd, 1971
1639. What is the area of Qatar?
    4,472 sq mi / 11,586 km²
1640. How long is the coastline of Qatar?
    350 mi / 563 km
1641. What is the population of Qatar?
    2,042,444 (by 2013)
1642. What is the currency of Qatar?
    Riyal

1643. What is the geographical feature of the terrain of Qatar?
Mostly flat and barren desert covered with loose sand and gravel

1644. What is the highest point of Qatar?
Qurayn Abu al Bawl (338 ft / 103 m)

1645. What is the lowest point of Qatar?
Persian Gulf (0 ft / 0 m)

1646. What is the inlet of the Persian Gulf in southeastern Qatar?
Khawr al Udayd, (also called Khor al Adaid, or Inland Sea)

1647. Why is the Halul Island, immediately off the east coast of Qatar, important?
Because it serves as a storage area and loading terminal for oil from the surrounding offshore fields

1648. The Hawar Islands, immediately off the west coast of Qatar, are the subject of a territorial dispute between Qatar and which country?
Bahrain

1649. What is Qatar's first and only national park, which consists of a few small islands surrounded by mudflats on the north-eastern tip of Qatar?
Umm Tais National Park

1650. What are administrative divisions called in Qatar?
Municipalities

1651. How many municipalities does Qatar have?
10

1652. What is the climate of Qatar?
Arid; mild, pleasant winters; very hot, humid summers

1653. What are the natural resources of Qatar?
Petroleum, natural gas, and fish

1654. What are the natural hazards of Qatar?
Haze, dust storms, sandstorms common

1655. What are the religions of Qatar?
Muslim 77.5%, Christian 8.5%, other 14%

1656. What are the ethnic groups of Qatar?
Arab 40%, Indian 18%, Pakistani 18%, Iranian 10%, other 14%

Saudi Arabia

1657. What is the official name of Saudi Arabia?
Kingdom of Saudi Arabia

1658. Which countries border Saudi Arabia to the north?
Jordan, Iraq, and Kuwait

1659. Which countries border Saudi Arabia to the east?
Qatar, Bahrain and the United Arab Emirates

1660. Which country borders Saudi Arabia to the southeast?
Oman

1661. Which country borders Saudi Arabia to the south?
Yemen

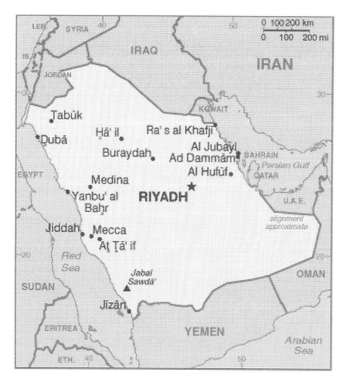
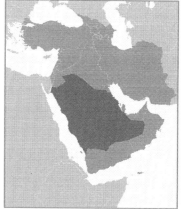

1662. Which body of water lies to the west of Saudi Arabia?
Red Sea

1663. Which body of water lies to the east of Saudi Arabia?
Persian Gulf

1664. What is the motto of Saudi Arabia?
There is no god other than Allah, and Muhammad is his messenger

1665. What is the national anthem of Saudi Arabia?
Long Live the King

1666. What is the capital of Saudi Arabia?
Riyadh (the largest city)

1667. What is the official language of Saudi Arabia?
Arabic

1668. What type of government does Saudi Arabia have?
Islamic Absolute Monarchy

1669. Why is Saudi Arabia called "The Land of the Two Holy Mosques"?
It refers to Mecca and Medina, the two holiest places in Islam. The two mosques are Masjid al-Haram in Mecca and Masjid Al-Nabawi in Medina

1670. The First Saudi State, which existed during 1744 – 1818, was the result of what religion movement?
Wahhabi movement, a fundamentalist/revisionist movement

1671. What was the Ottoman-Saudi War (also called Egyptian-Wahhabi War) during 1811 – 1818?
It was a war fought between Egypt (under Ottoman rule) and the First Saudi State, which ended with the Ottoman victory and the end of the First Saudi State

1672. During which period did the Second Saudi State exist?

116

1824 – 1891

1673. How was the Second Saudi different from the First Saudi State?
Less territorial expansion and less religious zeal

1674. When was the modern Saudi state founded by unifying most of the Arabian Peninsula?
September 23rd, 1932

1675. What discovery transformed Saudi Arabia on March 3rd, 1938?
Oil

1676. What is the area of Saudi Arabia?
829,780 sq mi / 2,149,690 km^2

1677. What is Saudi Arabia's rank by size among Arab countries of Middle East?
Largest

1678. Saudi Arabia occupies what percentage of Arabian Peninsula?
80%

1679. How long is the coastline of Saudi Arabia?
1,640 mi / 2,640 km

1680. What is the population of Saudi Arabia?
26,939,583 (by 2013)

1681. What is the currency of Saudi Arabia?
Saudi Riyal

1682. What is the geographical feature of the terrain of Saudi Arabia?
Mostly uninhabited, sandy desert

1683. What is the highest point of Saudi Arabia?
Jabal Sawda' (10,279 ft / 3,133 m)

1684. What is the lowest point of Saudi Arabia?
Persian Gulf (0 ft / 0 m)

1685. What is the Well of Zamzam?
It is a well located in Mecca; according to Islamic belief, it was a miraculously-generated source of water from God

1686. Where in Saudi Arabia are there coral reefs?
The coastal area by the Red Sea

1687. What is Saudi Arabia's ranking by oil reserves in the world?
Largest (264,100,000,000 Barrels)

1688. What is the only national park in Saudi Arabia, which includes Jabal Sawda'?
Asir National Park (618 sq mi / 1,600 km^2)

1689. What are administrative divisions called in Saudi Arabia?
Provinces

1690. How many provinces does Saudi Arabia have?
13

1691. What is the climate of Saudi Arabia?
Harsh, dry desert with great temperature extremes

1692. What are the natural resources of Saudi Arabia?
Petroleum, natural gas, iron ore, gold, and copper

1693. What are the natural hazards of Saudi Arabia?
Frequent sand and dust storms

1694. What are the religions of Saudi Arabia?

Arab 90%, Afro-Asian 10%

1695. What are the ethnic groups of Saudi Arabia?
Arab 90%, Afro-Asian 10%

Singapore

1696. What is the official name of Singapore?
Republic of Singapore

1697. Singapore is an island country off the southern tip of which peninsula?
Malay Peninsula

1698. Singapore is separated from Malaysia by which body of water to its north?
Straits of Johor

1699. Singapore is separated from Indonesia's Riau Islands by which body of water to its south?
Singapore Strait

1700. How many islands are there in Singapore, including the Singapore main island?
63

1701. What is the motto of Singapore?
Onward, Singapore

1702. What is the national anthem of Singapore?
Onward, Singapore

1703. What is the capital of Singapore?
Singapore

1704. What are the official languages of Singapore?
English and Malay

1705. What type of government does Singapore have?

Parliamentary Republic

1706. When was Singapore founded as a British (East India Company) protectorate?
February 6th, 1819

1707. Singapore was occupied by which country during February 15th, 1942 – September 12th, 1945?
Japan

1708. When did Singapore gain independence from the United Kingdom?
August 31st, 1963

1709. When did Singapore merge with Malaysia?
September 16th, 1963

1710. When did Singapore separate from Malaysia?
August 9th, 1965

1711. What is the area of Singapore?
269 sq mi / 697 km^2

1712. How long is the coastline of Singapore?
120 mi / 193 km

1713. What is the population of Singapore?
5,460,302 (by 2013)

1714. What is the currency of Singapore?
Singapore Dollar

1715. What is the geographical feature of the terrain of Singapore?
Lowland; gently undulating central plateau contains water catchment area and nature preserve

1716. What is the highest point of Singapore?
Bukit Timah (545 ft / 166 m)

1717. Bukit Timah is located on which island?
The Singapore main island

1718. What is the lowest point of Singapore?
Singapore Strait (0 ft / 0 m)

1719. About how many rivers are there in Singapore?
90

1720. What is the longest river in Singapore?
Kallang River (6 mi / 10 km)

1721. What is the Singapore River famous for?
The colorful and romantic history of the river and the myths and legends

1722. How long is Johor-Singapore Causeway, a causeway that links the city of Johor Bahru in Malaysia across the Straits of Johor to Singapore?
3,465 ft/ 1,056 m

1723. How long is Malaysia-Singapore Second Link (also called Tuas Second Link), a causeway that links the city of Johor Bahru in Malaysia across the Straits of Johor to Singapore?
6,299 ft / 1,920 m

1724. What is the climate of Singapore?
Tropical; hot, humid, rainy; two distinct monsoon seasons - Northeastern monsoon (December to March) and Southwestern monsoon (June to September); inter-monsoon - frequent afternoon and early evening thunderstorms

1725. What are the natural resources of Singapore?
Fish and deepwater ports

1726. What are the religions of Singapore?
Buddhist 42.5%, Muslim 14.9%, Taoist 8.5%, Hindu 4%, Catholic 4.8%, other Christian 9.8%, other 0.7%, none 14.8%

Sri Lanka

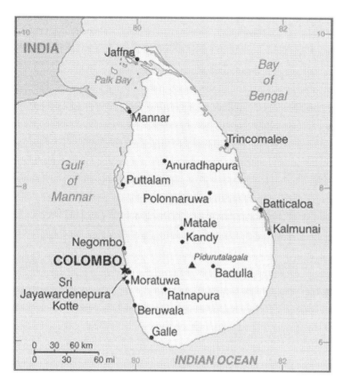

1727. What are the ethnic groups of Singapore?
Chinese 76.8%, Malay 13.9%, Indian 7.9%, other 1.4%

1728. What is the official name of Sri Lanka?
Democratic Socialist Republic of Sri Lanka

1729. Sri Lanka is off the southern coast of which country?
India

1730. What is the national anthem of Sri Lanka?
Mother Sri Lanka

1731. What is the capital of Sri Lanka?
Colombo (the largest city)

1732. What is the administrative capital of Sri Lanka?
Sri Jayawardenapura Kotte

1733. What are the official languages of Sri Lanka?
Sinhala and Tamil

1734. What type of government does Sri Lanka have?
Democratic Socialist Republic

1735. In the 14th century, a southern Indian dynasty established which kingdom in northern Ceylon?
Tamil

1736. Ceylon was ceded to whom in 1796?
United Kingdom

1737. When did Ceylon gain independence from the United Kingdom?
February 4th, 1948

1738. When did Ceylon become the Republic of Sri Lanka?
May 22nd, 1972

1739. When did Republic of Sri Lanka become the Democratic Socialist Republic of Sri Lanka?
September 7th, 1978

1740. What is the area of Sri Lanka?
25,325 sq mi / 65,610 km^2

1741. How long is the coastline of Sri Lanka?
833 mi / 1,340 km

1742. What is the population of Sri Lanka?
21,675,648 (by 2013)

1743. What is the currency of Sri Lanka?
Sri Lankan Rupee

1744. What is the geographical feature of the terrain of Sri Lanka?
Mostly low, flat to rolling plain; mountains in south-central interior

1745. What is the highest point of Sri Lanka?
Pidurutalagala (8,281 ft / 2,524 m)

1746. What is the lowest point of Sri Lanka?
Indian Ocean (0 ft / 0 m)

1747. What is Rama's Bridge (also called Adam's Bridge or Rama Setu)?
It was a land connection from Sri Lanka to the Indian mainland; according to temple records this natural causeway was formerly complete during the rule of Rama, but was breached by a violent storm (probably a cyclone) in 1480

1748. What is special about Adam's Peak (7,359 ft / 2,243 m)?
It is well-known for the Sri Pada "sacred footprint", a 5.9 ft (1.8 m) rock formation near the summit; in Buddhist tradition it is the footprint of the Buddha; in Hindu tradition it is for Shiva; in Muslim tradition it is for Adam

1749. What is the longest river in Sri Lanka?
Mahaweli River (208 mi / 335 km)

1750. What is the source of the Mahaweli River?
Adam's Peak

1751. What is the mouth of the Mahaweli River?
Bay of Bengal

1752. What is the second longest river in Sri Lanka?
Malvathu River (102 mi / 164 km)

1753. Which national parks are located in Sri Lanka?
Maduru Oya National Park, Somawathiya National Park, Wasgamuwa National Park, Wilpattu National Park, Udawalawe National Park, Gal Oya National Park, Lunugamvehera National Park, Kumana National Park, Flood Plains National Park, Minneriya National Park,

Angammedilla National Park, Kaudulla National Park, Bundala National Park, Horton Plains National Park, Lahugala Kitulana National Park, Pigeon Island National Park, Hikkaduwa National Park, Galway's Land National Park, Yala National Park, and Horagolla National Park

1754. What is the largest national park in Sri Lanka, located in western area, which has nearly 60 natural, sand-rimmed water basins or depressions that fill with rainwater?
Wilpattu National Park (508 sq mi / 1,317 km^2)

1755. What is the second largest and most visited national park in Sri Lanka, located in southern area, which is famous for its variety of its wild animals?
Yala National Park (378 sq mi / 979 km^2)

1756. What are administrative divisions called in Sri Lanka?
Provinces

1757. How many provinces does Sri Lanka have?
9

1758. What is the climate of Sri Lanka?
Tropical monsoon; northeast monsoon (December to March); southwest monsoon (June to October)

1759. What are the natural resources of Sri Lanka?
Limestone, graphite, mineral sands, gems, phosphates, clay, and hydropower

1760. What are the natural hazards of Sri Lanka?
Occasional cyclones and tornadoes

1761. What are the religions of Sri Lanka?
Buddhist 69.1%, Muslim 7.6%, Hindu 7.1%, Christian 6.2%, unspecified 10%

1762. What are the ethnic groups of Sri Lanka?
Sinhalese 73.8%, Sri Lankan Moors 7.2%, Indian Tamil 4.6%, Sri Lankan Tamil 3.9%, other 0.5%, unspecified 10%

Syria

1763. What is the official name of Syria?
Syrian Arab Republic

1764. Which country borders Syria to the southwest?
Israel

1765. Which country borders Syria to the west?
Lebanon

1766. Which country borders Syria to the north?
Turkey

1767. Which country borders Syria to the east?
Iraq

1768. Which country borders Syria to the south?
Jordan

1769. Which body of water lies to the west of Syria?
Mediterranean Sea

1770. What is the national anthem of Syria?
Guardians of the Land

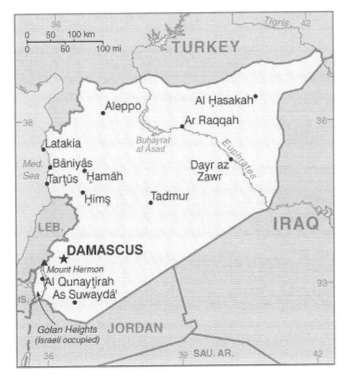 

1771. What is the capital of Syria?
Damascus (the largest city)

1772. What is the official language of Syria?
Arabic

1773. What type of government does Syria have?
Republic under an Authoritarian Military-dominated Regime

1774. Syria has been part of which empires before its independence on September 30th, 1918?
Egyptian Empire, Assyrian Empire, Babylonian Empire, Persian Empire, Seleucid Empire, Roman Empire, Byzantine Empire, Seljuq Empire, and Ottoman Empire

1775. When did Syria become a League of Nations Mandate under France?
September 29th, 1923

1776. When did Syria gain independence from the League of Nations Mandate under France?
April 17th, 1946

1777. Syria and which country formed the United Arab Republic on February 22nd, 1958?
Egypt

1778. When was the United Arab Republic disestablished, and the Syrian Arab Republic was reestablished?
September 28th, 1961

1779. When did Israel occupy Golan Heights?
June 10th, 1967 (following the Six-Day War)

1780. What is the area of Syria?
71,479 sq mi / 185,180 km^2

1781. How long is the coastline of Syria?
120 mi / 193 km

1782. What is the population of Syria?
22,457,336 (by 2013)
1783. What is the currency of Syria?
Syrian Pound
1784. What is the geographical feature of the terrain of Syria?
Primarily semiarid and desert plateau; narrow coastal plain; mountains in west
1785. What is the highest point of Syria?
Mount Hermon (9,232 ft / 2,814 m)
1786. Where is Mount Hermon located?
Israeli-occupied Golan Heights
1787. Mount Hermon is located in which mountain range?
Anti-Lebanon mountains (also called Eastern Lebanon Mountain Range)
1788. What is the Homs Gap (also called Akkar Gap)?
It is a relatively flat passage in the Orontes River Valley of southern Syria
1789. What is the lowest point of Syria?
Unnamed location near Lake Tiberias (-656 ft / -200 m)
1790. The Syrian Desert (also called Syro-Arabian Desert) covers potions of which countries?
Syria, Iraq, Jordan and Saudi Arabia
1791. What is the longest river in Syria, which bisects the Syrian Desert and is located in Iraq, Syria, and Turkey?
Euphrates River (2,234 mi / 3,596 km)
1792. What is the largest lake in Syria?
Lake Assad (203 sq mi / 525 km^2)
1793. Lake Assad is a reservoir, created by the construction of the Tabqa Dam on which river?
Euphrates River
1794. What is the highest point of Jabal al-Druze, an elevated volcanic region in southern Syria?
Tell Qeni (5,915 ft / 1,803 m)
1795. What is the highest point of the An-Nusayriyah Mountains (also called al-Alawiyeen Mountains, Coastal Mountain Range), a mountain range in northwestern Syria running north to south?
Nabi Yunis (5,125 ft / 1,562 m)
1796. What is the Hauran Plateau?
It is a volcanic plateau in southwestern Syria and extending into the northwestern corner of Jordan
1797. What are administrative divisions called in Syria?
Provinces
1798. How many provinces does Syria have?
14
1799. What is the climate of Syria?
Mostly desert; hot, dry, sunny summers (June to August) and mild, rainy winters (December to February) along coast; cold weather with snow or sleet periodically in Damascus
1800. What are the natural resources of Syria?
Petroleum, phosphates, chrome and manganese ores, asphalt, iron ore, rock salt, marble, gypsum, and hydropower
1801. What are the natural hazards of Syria?

Dust storms and sandstorms

1802. What are the religions of Syria?
Sunni Muslim 74%, other Muslim (includes Alawite, Druze) 16%, Christian (various denominations) 10%, Jewish (tiny communities in Damascus, Al Qamishli, and Aleppo)

1803. What are the ethnic groups of Syria?
Arab 90.3%, Kurds, Armenians, and other 9.7%

Taiwan (China)

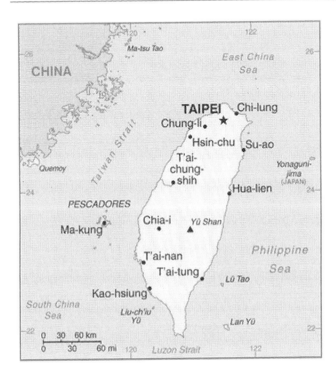

1804. What are other names of Taiwan?
Formosa and Republic of China

1805. Taiwan is located at which direction of mainland China?
Southeast

1806. Taiwan is located at which direction of the Philippines?
North

1807. Which body of water separates Taiwan from China?
Taiwan Strait

1808. Which body of water separates Taiwan from the Philippines?
Luzon Strait

1809. Which body of water lies to the east of Taiwan?
Philippine Sea

1810. Which body of water lies to the north of Taiwan?
East China Sea

1811. Which body of water lies to the south of Taiwan?
South China Sea

1812. Besides the Taiwan Island, which other islands are a part of Taiwan?
Orchid Island, Penghu islands, Green Island, Hsiao Liuchiu, Kinmen, Matsu, Wuchiu, Pratas and Taiping

1813. What is the capital of Taiwan?
Taipei (the largest city)

1814. What is the official language of Taiwan?
Chinese

1815. What type of government does Taiwan have?
Multiparty Democracy

1816. In which year did a Portuguese ship sighted the main island of Taiwan and named it Ilha Formosa?
1544

1817. When did Tainan (southern Taiwan) become a Dutch colony under the name of Tayowan?
August 26th, 1624

1818. When did northern Taiwan become a Spanish colony under the name of Isla Hermosa?
May 7th, 1626

1819. When did the Dutch drive out the Spanish, and make Taiwan a Dutch colony?
August 25th, 1642

1820. When was Taiwan annexed by China?
May 27th, 1684

1821. When did China hand over Taiwan to Japan based on the Treaty of Shimonoseki (also called the Treaty of Maguan)?
May 8th, 1895

1822. When was Taiwan returned to Chinese control?
October 25th, 1945

1823. The Republic of China lost the Chinese Civil War to the Communist Party of China and was driven to Taiwan. When did Taiwan become the seat of Republic of China?
December 8th, 1949

1824. When was Republic of China expelled from the United Nations and replaced by the People's Republic of China?
November 15th, 1971

1825. What is the area of Taiwan?
13,888 sq mi / 35,980 km^2

1826. How long is the coastline of Taiwan?
973 mi / 1,566 km

1827. What is the population of Taiwan?
23,299,716 (by 2013)

1828. What is the currency of Taiwan?
New Taiwan Dollar

1829. What is the geographical feature of the terrain of Taiwan?
Eastern two-thirds mostly rugged mountains; flat to gently rolling plains in west

1830. What is the highest point of Taiwan?
Yu Shan (12,966 ft / 3,952 m)

1831. What is the lowest point of Taiwan?
South China Sea (0 ft / 0 m)

1832. What is the longest river in Taiwan?
Zhuoshui River (116 mi / 186 km)

1833. What is the largest lake in Taiwan?
Sun Moon Lake (3 sq mi / 8 km^2)

1834. Which national parks are located in Taiwan?
Dongsha Marine National Park, Kenting National Park, Kinmen National Park, Shei-Pa National Park, Taroko National Park, Yangmingshan National Park, and Yushan National Park

1835. What is the largest national park in Taiwan, located on Dongsha Islands, which is home to 72 species of endemic plants and 125 species of insects?
Dongsha Marine National Park (1,365 sq mi / 3537 km^2)

1836. What is the second largest national park in Taiwan, located in central Taiwan, which contains the highest peak of Taiwan?
Yushan National Park (407 sq mi / 1055 km^2)

1837. What is the third largest national park in Taiwan, located in eastern Taiwan, which is famous for marble gorge?
Taroko National Park (355 sq mi / 920 km^2)

1838. What are administrative divisions called in Taiwan?
Counties

1839. How many counties does Taiwan have?
18 (plus 5 municipalities and 2 special municipalities)

1840. What is the climate of Taiwan?
Tropical; marine; rainy season during southwest monsoon (June to August); cloudiness is persistent and extensive all year

1841. What are the natural resources of Taiwan?
Small deposits of coal, natural gas, limestone, marble, and asbestos

1842. What are the natural hazards of Taiwan?
Earthquakes and typhoons

1843. What are the religions of Taiwan?
Mixture of Buddhist and Taoist 93%, Christian 4.5%, other 2.5%

1844. What are the ethnic groups of Taiwan?
Taiwanese (including Hakka) 84%, mainland Chinese 14%, indigenous 2%

Tajikistan

1845. What is the official name of Tajikistan?
Republic of Tajikistan

1846. Which country borders Tajikistan to the south?
Afghanistan

1847. Which country borders Tajikistan to the west and north?
Uzbekistan

1848. Which country borders Tajikistan to the north?
Kyrgyzstan

1849. Which country borders Tajikistan to the east?
China

1850. What is the national anthem of Tajikistan?
National Anthem of Tajikistan

1851. What is the capital of Tajikistan?
Dushanbe (the largest city)

1852. What is the official language of Tajikistan?
Tajik

1853. What type of government does Tajikistan have?
Unitary Semi-presidential Republic

1854. When did Russia annex Tajikistan?
June 30th, 1868

1855. When did Tajikistan become the Tadzikh Autonomous Republic within Uzbekistan?
March 15th, 1925

1856. When did Tajikistan become the Tadzikh Soviet Socialist Republic within Soviet Union?
December 5th, 1929

1857. When did Tajikistan gain independence from the Soviet Union?
September 9th, 1991

1858. What was the Civil War in Tajikistan during May 1992 – June 27, 1997?
It was a civil war that involved various factions fighting one another due to clan loyalties; it ended with a United Nations-sponsored armistice; it resulted in over 100,000 deaths

1859. What is the area of Tajikistan?
55,237 sq mi / 143,100 km^2

1860. How long is the coastline of Tajikistan?
0 mi / 0 km (landlocked)

1861. What is the population of Tajikistan?
7,910,041 (by 2013)

1862. What is the currency of Tajikistan?
Somoni

1863. What is the geographical feature of the terrain of Tajikistan?
Pamir and Alay Mountains dominate landscape; western Fergana Valley in north, Kofarnihon and Vakhsh Valleys in southwest

1864. What percentage of Tajikistan is covered by mountains?
93%

1865. What is the highest point of Tajikistan?
Qullai Ismoili Somoni (also called Communism Peak, 24,590 ft / 7,495 m)

1866. What was Qullai Ismoili Somoni's rank by height in the Soviet Union?
1st

1867. Qullai Ismoili Somoni is located in which mountain range?
Pamirs Mountains

1868. What is the second highest point of Tajikistan, located in the Trans-Alay Range of Pamirs Mountains?
Pik Lenin (23,406 ft / 7,134 m)

1869. What is the third highest point of Tajikistan, located in the Akademiya Nauk Range of Pamirs Mountains?
Pik Korzhenevskaya (23,310 ft / 7,105 m)

1870. What is the longest glacier in the world outside the polar regions, located on Mount Garmo of Pamirs Mountains?
Fedchenko Glacier (48 mi / 77 km)

1871. Which mountain ranges are located in the Pamir-Alay mountain system of Tajikistan?
Alay Mountains, Zarafshan Range, Turkestan Range, and Gissar Range

1872. What is the lowest point of Tajikistan?
Syr Darya (984 ft / 300 m)

1873. What is the longest river in Tajikistan, which flows through Tajikistan and Uzbekistan?
Zeravshan River (also called Zarafshon, 485 mi / 781 km, Tajikistan: 196 mi / 316 km)

1874. What is the second longest river in Tajikistan, which flows through Kazakhstan, Kyrgyzstan, Uzbekistan and Tajikistan?
Syr Darya (1,374 mi / 2,212 km, Tajikistan: 121 mi / 195 km)

1875. What is the largest lake in Tajikistan?
Karakul (also called Qaraqul, endorheic, 147 sq mi / 380 km²)

1876. What is the second largest lake in Tajikistan?
Kayrakum Reservoir (artificial)

1877. What are national parks in Tajikistan?

Pamir National Park, Shirkent National Park, and Tajikistan National Park
1878. What are administrative divisions called in Tajikistan?
Provinces
1879. How many provinces does Tajikistan have?
2 (plus 1 autonomous province)
1880. What is the climate of Tajikistan?
Mid-latitude continental, hot summers, mild winters; semiarid to polar in Pamir Mountains
1881. What are the natural resources of Tajikistan?
Hydropower, some petroleum, uranium, mercury, brown coal, lead, zinc, antimony, tungsten, silver, and gold
1882. What are the natural hazards of Tajikistan?
Earthquakes and floods
1883. What are the religions of Tajikistan?
Sunni Muslim 85%, Shia Muslim 5%, other 10%
1884. What are the ethnic groups of Tajikistan?
Tajik 79.9%, Uzbek 15.3%, Russian 1.1%, Kyrgyz 1.1%, other 2.6%

Thailand

1885. What is the official name of Thailand?
Kingdom of Thailand
1886. Which country borders Thailand to the south?
Malaysia
1887. Which country borders Thailand to the north and east?
Laos
1888. Which country borders Thailand to the north and west?
Burma
1889. Which country borders Thailand to the east?
Cambodia
1890. What is the Kra Isthmus?
A narrow land bridge which connects Malay Peninsula with the mainland of Asia
1891. What is the nickname of the Kra Isthmus?
The Devil's Neck
1892. Which body of water lies to the east of the Kra Isthmus?
Gulf of Thailand
1893. Which body of water lies to the west of the Kra Isthmus?
Andaman Sea
1894. What is the national anthem of Thailand?
Thai National Anthem
1895. What is the capital of Thailand?
Bangkok (the largest city)
1896. What is the official language of Thailand?
Thai
1897. What type of government does Thailand have?
Constitutional Monarchy

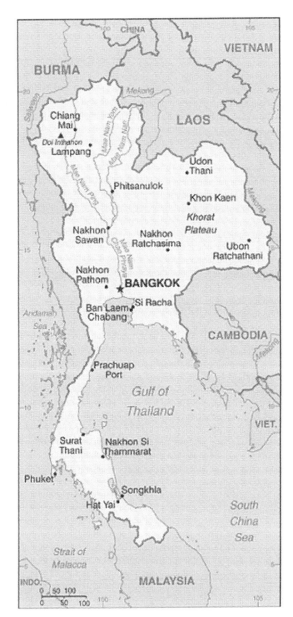

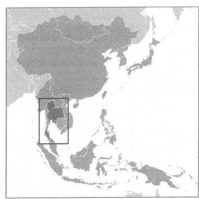

1898. Over the years until 1939, which kingdoms were established in Thailand?
Sukhothai Kingdom, Ayutthaya Kingdom, Thonburi Kingdom, and the Rattanakosin Kingdom

1899. When did a bloodless revolution lead to a constitutional monarchy in Thailand?
June 24th, 1932

1900. When was the Kingdom of Thailand established to replace the name, Siam?
June 23rd, 1939

1901. Thailand was allied with which country during December 8th, 1941 – August 15th, 1945
Japan

1902. What is the area of Thailand?
198,064 sq mi / 513,120 km^2

1903. How long is the coastline of Thailand?

2,000 mi / 3,219 km

1904. What is the population of Thailand?
67,448,120 (by 2013)

1905. What is the currency of Thailand?
Baht

1906. What is the geographical feature of the terrain of Thailand?
Central plain; Khorat Plateau in the east; mountains elsewhere

1907. What is the highest point of Thailand?
Doi Inthanon (8,451 ft / 2,576 m)

1908. Doi Inthanon is located in which mountain range?
Shan Hills

1909. What is the lowest point of Thailand?
Gulf of Thailand (0 ft / 0 m)

1910. What are two principal river systems of Thailand?
Chao Phraya (231 mi / 372 km) and Mekong

1911. What is the longest river in Thailand?
Chi River (475 mi / 765 km)

1912. What is the second longest river in Thailand?
Mun River (466 mi / 750 km)

1913. Which river carries more water, the Chi River or the Mun River?
Mun River

1914. What is the largest lake in Thailand?
Songkhla Lake (401 sq mi / 1,040 km²)

1915. What is the second largest lake in Thailand?
Bueng Boraphet (86 sq mi / 224 km²)

1916. What is the third largest lake in Thailand?
Nong Han Lake (48 sq mi / 125 km²)

1917. Which national parks are located in Thailand?
Ao Phang Nga (Phang Nga Bay) National Park, Chiang Dao National Park, Erawan National Park, Hat Khanom - Mu Ko Thale Tai National Park, Kaeng Chet Khwae National Park, Kaeng Krachan National Park, Kaeng Krung National Park, Khao Laem Ya - Mu Ko Samet National Park, Khao Phra Wihan National Park, Khao Sam Roi Yot National Park, Khao Luang National Park, Khao Sok National Park, Khao Yai National Park, Khlong Lan National Park, Khlong Phanom National Park, Khlong Wang Chao National Park, Kui Buri National Park, Mae Yom National Park, Mae Wong National Park, Mu Ko Ang Thong National Park, Mu Ko Lanta National Park, Mu Ko Phetra National Park, Mu Ko Surin National Park, Namtok Chat Trakan National Park, Pa Hin Ngam National Park, Pha Taem National Park, Phu Hin Rong Kla National Park, Phu Kradueng National Park, Ramkhamhaeng National Park, Si Phang-nga National Park, Si Satchanalai National Park, Similan Islands National Park, Tai Rom Yen National Park, Tarutao (Marine) National Park, Thale Ban National Park, Than Sadet-Ko Pha-Ngan National Park, and Thung Salaeng Luang National Park

1918. What is the largest national park in Thailand, located in central Thailand, which consists mainly of rain forests within the eastern slope of the Tenasserim Mountain Range?
Kaeng Krachan National Park (1,125 sq mi / 2,915 km²)

1919. What is the second largest national park in Thailand, located in northeastern Thailand,

which consists of big and small mountains, valleys, chasms and waterfalls?
Thab Lan National Park (863 sq mi / 2,236 km²)

1920. What is the third largest national park in Thailand, located in northeastern Thailand, which consists of evergreen forests and grasslands?
Khao Yai National Park (837 sq mi / 2,168 km²)

1921. What are administrative divisions called in Thailand?
Provinces

1922. How many provinces does Thailand have?
76

1923. What is the climate of Thailand?
Tropical; rainy, warm, cloudy southwest monsoon (mid-May to September); dry, cool northeast monsoon (November to mid-March); southern isthmus always hot and humid

1924. What are the natural resources of Thailand?
Tin, rubber, natural gas, tungsten, tantalum, timber, lead, fish, gypsum, lignite, fluorite, and arable land

1925. What are the natural hazards of Thailand?
Land subsidence in Bangkok area resulting from the depletion of the water table; droughts

1926. What are the religions of Thailand?
Buddhist 94.6%, Muslim 4.6%, Christian 0.7%, other 0.1%

1927. What are the ethnic groups of Thailand?
Thai 75%, Chinese 14%, other 11%

Timor-Leste

1928. What is the official name of Timor-Leste?
Democratic Republic of Timor-Leste
1929. What is the common name of Timor-Leste?
East Timor
1930. Timor-Leste shares the island of Timor with which country?
Indonesia
1931. Timor-Leste is the only Asian country that lies entirely south of which imaginary line?
Equator
1932. What is the motto of Timor-Leste?
Unity, Action, Progress
1933. What is the national anthem of Timor-Leste?
Fatherland
1934. What is the capital of Timor-Leste?
Dili (the largest city)
1935. What are the official languages of Timor-Leste?
Tetum and Portuguese
1936. What type of government does Timor-Leste have?
Parliamentary Republic
1937. Timor-Leste became whose colony in 1642?
Portuguese
1938. Who occupied Timor-Leste during February 20th, 1942 – September 11th, 1945?
Japan
1939. When did Timor-Leste gain independence from Portugal?
November 28th, 1975
1940. When was Timor-Leste occupied by Indonesia?
December 7th, 1975
1941. When did Timor-Leste gain independence from Indonesia?
May 20th, 2002
1942. What is the area of Timor-Leste?
5,741 sq mi / 14,874 km^2
1943. How long is the coastline of Timor-Leste?
439 mi / 706 km
1944. What is the population of Timor-Leste?
1,172,390 (by 2013)
1945. What is the currency of Timor-Leste?
U.S. Dollar
1946. What is the geographical feature of the terrain of Timor-Leste?
Mountainous
1947. What is the highest point of Timor-Leste?
Foho Tatamailau (9,721 ft / 2,963 m)
1948. What is the lowest point of Timor-Leste?
Timor Sea, Savu Sea, and Banda Sea (0 ft / 0 m)
1949. What is the first and only national park in Timor-Leste, which links three important bird areas: Lore, Monte Paitchau, Lake Iralalara, and Jaco Island?
Nino Konis Santana National Park (477 sq mi / 1,236 km²)

1950. What are administrative divisions called in Timor-Leste?

Administrative districts

1951. How many administrative districts does Timor-Leste have?

13

1952. What is the climate of Timor-Leste?

Tropical; hot, humid; distinct rainy and dry seasons

1953. What are the natural resources of Timor-Leste?

Gold, petroleum, natural gas, manganese, and marble

1954. What are the natural hazards of Timor-Leste?

Floods and landslides are common; earthquakes; tsunamis; tropical cyclones

1955. What are the religions of Timor-Leste?

Roman Catholic 98%, Muslim 1%, Protestant 1%

1956. What are the ethnic groups of Timor-Leste?

Austronesian (Malayo-Polynesian), Papuan, small Chinese minority

Turkey

1957. What is the official name of Turkey?
Republic of Turkey

1958. Which country borders Turkey to the northwest?
Bulgaria

1959. Which country borders Turkey to the west?
Greece

1960. Which country borders Turkey to the northeast?
Georgia

1961. Which countries border Turkey to the south?
Iraq and Syria

1962. Which countries border Turkey to the east?
Armenia, Azerbaijan (the exclave of Nakhchivan) and Iran

1963. Which body of water lies to the south of Turkey?
Mediterranean Sea

1964. Which body of water lies to the west of Turkey?
Aegean Sea

1965. Which body of water lies to the north of Turkey?
Black Sea

1966. What is the European part of Turkey called?
Eastern Thrace (also called Turkish Thrace, European Turkey)

1967. What is the Asian part of Turkey called?
Anatolia (also called Asia Minor)

1968. Which lines separate Eastern Thrace and Anatolia?
Sea of Marmara and Turkish Straits (Bosphorus Strait and Dardanelles Strait)

1969. What is the motto of Turkey?
Peace at Home, Peace in the World

1970. What is the national anthem of Turkey?
The Anthem of Independence

1971. What is the capital of Turkey?
Ankara

1972. What is the largest city of Turkey?
Istanbul

1973. Istanbul (also known as Constantinople) was the capital of which empires?
Roman Empire (330–395), Eastern Roman (Byzantine) Empire (395–1204 and 1261–1453), Latin Empire (1204–1261), and Ottoman Empire (1453–1922)

1974. What is the official language of Turkey?
Turkish

1975. What type of government does Turkey have?
Republican Parliamentary Democracy

1976. During which period did the Ottoman Empire exist?
1299 – 1923

1977. What was the official name of the Ottoman Empire?
Sublime Ottoman State

1978. What were capitals of the Ottoman Empire?

Sogut (1302–1326), Bursa (1326–1365), Edirne (1365–1453), and Istanbul (1453–1922)

1979. What type of government was the Ottoman Empire?
Monarchy

1980. What was the area of the Ottoman Empire in 1595?
7,683,433 sq mi / 19,900,000 km^2

1981. What present-day countries or territories totally or partially belonged to the Ottoman Empire?
Albania, Algeria, Armenia, Austria, Azerbaijan, Bosnia and Herzegovina, Bulgaria, Croatia, Cyprus, Egypt, Eritrea, Ethiopia, Georgia, Greece, Hungary, Iran, Iraq, Israel, Jordan, Kuwait, Lebanon, Libya, Macedonia, Moldov, Montenegro, Palestinian territories, Romania, Russia, Saudi Arabia, Serbia, Slovakia, Slovenia, Somalia, Sudan, Syria, Tunisia, Turkey, Ukraine, and Yemen

1982. What happened to the Ottoman Empire after World War I?
Most of the Anatolia and Eastern Thrace was occupied by the Allies, including Istanbul

1983. How was the Ottoman Empire partitioned following the Treaty of Sèvres, signed on August 10th, 1920?
League of Nations granted France mandates over Syria and Lebanon, and granted the United Kingdom mandates over Mesopotamia and Palestine; parts of the Ottoman Empire on the Arabian Peninsula became parts of what are the present-day Saudi Arabia and Yemen

1984. What was the Turkish War of Independence during May 19th, 1919 – October 29th, 1923?
It was a war of independence waged by Turkish Nationalists against the Allies; a decisive Turkish Victory; overthrew the Ottoman Sultanate; established of Republic of Turkey

1985. When was Republic of Turkey established?
October 29th, 1923

1986. What is the area of Turkey?
302,535 sq mi / 783,562 km^2

1987. How long is the coastline of Turkey?
4,474 mi / 7,200 km

1988. What is the population of Turkey?
80,694,485 (by 2013)

1989. What is the currency of Turkey?
Turkish Lira

1990. What is the geographical feature of the terrain of Turkey?
High central plateau (Anatolia); narrow coastal plain; several mountain ranges

1991. What is the highest point of Turkey?
Mount Ararat (16,949 ft / 5,166 m)

1992. Mount Ararat has which two peaks?
Greater Ararat (16,949 ft / 5,166 m) and Lesser Ararat (12,782 ft / 3,896 m)

1993. What type of mountain is Mount Ararat?
A snow-capped, dormant volcanic cone (stratovolcano)

1994. What was special about Mount Ararat, according to the book of Genesis?
It was the legendary landing place of Noah's ark

1995. What is the lowest point of Turkey?
Mediterranean Sea (0 ft / 0 m)

1996. What is the longest river in Turkey?

Kizilirmak River (also called Halys River, 840 mi / 1,350 km)

1997. What is the largest lake in Turkey?

Lake Van (1,450 sq mi /3,755 km^2)

1998. What are islands in Lake Van?

Akdamar, Charpanak, Lim, and Arter

1999. Which national parks are located in Turkey?

Yozgat Forest National Park, Karatepe-Arslantas National Park, Soguksu National Park, Kuscenneti National Park, Uludag National Park, Yedigoller National Park, Cape Dilek - Delta of Buyuk Menderes National Park, Spil Mount National Park, Mount Kizil National Park, Mount Gulluk National Park, Kovada Lake National Park, Munzur Valley National Park, Beydaglari Coast National Park, Gallipoli Peninsula Historical National Park, Koprulu Canyon National Park, Mount Ilgaz National Park, Historical Baskomutan National Park, Ancient Goreme National Park, Altindere Valley National Park, Ancient Bogazkoy Alacahoyuk National Park, Mount Nemrut National Park, Beysehir Lake National Park, Kazdagi National Park, Kackar Mountains National Park, Hatilla Valley National Park, Karagol-Sahara National Park, Altinbesik Cave National Park, Mount Honaz National Park, Aladaglar National Park, Marmaris National Park, Saklikent National Park, Ancient Troya National Park, and Kastamonu-Bartin Kure Mountains National Park

2000. What is the largest national park in Turkey, which is famous for its mountain peaks, alpine meadows, crystal clear lakes, and dense forests?

Kackar Mountains National Park (199 sq mi / 515 km^2)

2001. What are administrative divisions called in Turkey?

Provinces

2002. How many provinces does Turkey have?

81

2003. What is the climate of Turkey?

Temperate; hot, dry summers with mild, wet winters; harsher in interior

2004. What are the natural resources of Turkey?

Coal, iron ore, copper, chromium, antimony, mercury, gold, barite, borate, celestite (strontium), emery, feldspar, limestone, magnesite, marble, perlite, pumice, pyrites (sulfur), clay, arable land, and hydropower

2005. What are the natural hazards of Turkey?

Severe earthquakes, especially in northern Turkey, along an arc extending from the Sea of Marmara to Lake Van

2006. What are the religions of Turkey?

Muslim 99.8% (mostly Sunni), other 0.2% (mostly Christians and Jews)

2007. What are the ethnic groups of Turkey?

Turkish 70-75%, Kurdish 18%, other minorities 7-12%

Turkmenistan

2008. What is the official name of Turkmenistan?

Republic of Turkmenistan

2009. Which country borders Turkmenistan to the southeast?
Afghanistan

2010. Which country borders Turkmenistan to the south?
Iran

2011. Which country borders Turkmenistan to the north and east?
Uzbekistan

2012. Which country borders Turkmenistan to the north?
Kazakhstan

2013. Which body of water lies to the west of Turkmenistan?
Caspian Sea

2014. What is the national anthem of Turkmenistan?
National Anthem of Independent Neutral Turkmenistan

2015. What is the capital of Turkmenistan?
Ashgabat (the largest city)

2016. What is the official language of Turkmenistan?
Turkmen

2017. What type of government does Turkmenistan have?
Presidential Republic Single-party State

2018. Turkmenistan was gradually annexed by which country during 1869 – 1885?
Russia

2019. When did Turkmenistan become the Turkmen Soviet Socialist Republic?
October 27th, 1924

2020. When did Turkmenistan gain independence from the Soviet Union?
October 27th, 1991

2021. What is the area of Turkmenistan?
188,407 sq mi / 488,100 km^2
2022. How long is the coastline of Turkmenistan?
0 mi / 0 km (landlocked)
2023. What is the population of Turkmenistan?
5,113,040 (by 2013)
2024. What is the currency of Turkmenistan?
Turkmen New Manat
2025. What is the geographical feature of the terrain of Turkmenistan?
Flat-to-rolling sandy desert with dunes rising to mountains in the south; low mountains along border with Iran; borders Caspian Sea in west
2026. What is the highest point of Turkmenistan?
Gora Ayribaba (10,299 ft / 3,139 m)
2027. Gora Ayribaba is located in which mountain range?
Koytendag Range of Pamir-Alay mountain system
2028. What is the lowest point of Turkmenistan?
Vpadina Akchanaya (also called Sarygamysh Lake, -266 ft / -81 m)
2029. What is the elevation of Sarygamysh Koli, comparing to Vpadina Akchanaya?
Sarygamysh Koli's water level fluctuates above and below the elevation of Vpadina Akchanaya (the lake has dropped as low as -110 m)
2030. What is the largest lake of Turkmenistan, located in Turkmenistan and Uzbekistan?
Sarygamysh Lake (a dry lakebed from time to time)
2031. Whare are major rivers in Turkmenistan?
Atrek River, Tejen River (also called Harirud River), Morghab River, and Amu Darya
2032. What is the longest river in Turkmenistan, located in Afghanistan, Tajikistan, Turkmenistan, and Uzbekistan?
Amu Darya (1,600 mi / 2,574 km)
2033. What is the Qaraqum Canal?
It is a navigable canel over much of its 854 mi (1,375 km) length, and carries 3 cube mi (13 km^3) of water annually from Amu Darya
2034. Which reservoir is a component of Qaraqum Canal and was created to control the erratic Tejen River?
Hanhowuz Reservoir
2035. Which desert covers over 80% of Turkmenistan?
Karakum Desert (also called Garagum Desert)
2036. Karakum desert lies at the southern portion of which depression?
Turan Depression (also called Turan Lowland or Turanian Basin)
2037. What are administrative divisions called in Turkmenistan?
Provinces
2038. How many provinces does Turkmenistan have?
5 (plus 1 independent city)
2039. What is the climate of Turkmenistan?
Subtropical desert
2040. What are the natural resources of Turkmenistan?
Petroleum, natural gas, sulfur, and salt

2041. What are the religions of Turkmenistan?
    Muslim 89%, Eastern Orthodox 9%, unknown 2%
2042. What are the ethnic groups of Turkmenistan?
    Turkmen 85%, Uzbek 5%, Russian 4%, other 6%

United Arab Emirates

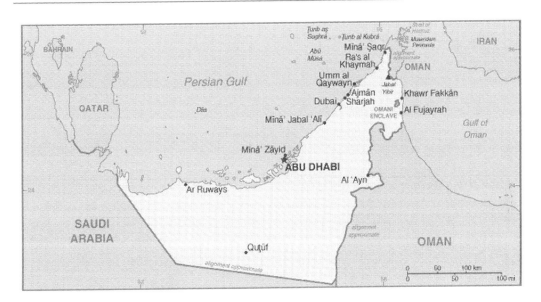

2043. Which country borders the United Arab Emirates to the west and South?
    Saudi Arabia
2044. Which country borders the United Arab Emirates to the east?
    Oman
2045. Which body of water lies to the east of the United Arab Emirates?
    Gulf of Oman
2046. Which body of water lies to the north of the United Arab Emirates?
    Persian Gulf
2047. What is the motto of the United Arab Emirates?
    God, Nation, President

2048. What is the national anthem of the United Arab Emirates?
Long Live my Nation

2049. What is the capital of the United Arab Emirates?
Abu Dhabi

2050. What is the largest city and largest natural harbor of the United Arab Emirates?
Dubai

2051. What is the official language of the United Arab Emirates?
Arabic

2052. What type of government does the United Arab Emirates have?
Federal Presidential System and Constitutional Monarchy

2053. When did the United Arab Emirates become the British protectorate of Trucial States (also called Trucial Oman)?
March 8th, 1892

2054. When did the United Arab Emirates gain independence from the United Kingdom?
December 2nd, 1971

2055. What is the area of the United Arab Emirates?
32,270 sq mi / 83,600 km^2

2056. How long is the coastline of the United Arab Emirates?
819 mi / 1,318 km

2057. What is the population of the United Arab Emirates?
5,473,972 (by 2013)

2058. What is the currency of the United Arab Emirates?
UAE Dirham

2059. What is the geographical feature of the terrain of the United Arab Emirates?
Flat, barren coastal plain merging into rolling sand dunes of vast desert wasteland; mountains in east

2060. What is the highest point of the United Arab Emirates?
Jabal Yibir (5,010 ft / 1,527 m)

2061. Jabal Yibir is located in which mountain range?
Al Hajar Mountains

2062. What is the lowest point of the United Arab Emirates?
Persian Gulf (0 ft / 0 m)

2063. Al Liwa Oasis, which has the largest sand dunes in the world, is on the northern edge of which desert, located in Saudi Arabia, Oman, United Arab Emirates, and Yemen?
Rub' al Khali Desert (also called Empty Quarter, 250,000 sq mi / 650,000 km^2)

2064. What is the only national park in the United Arab Emirates, located in northeastern the United Arab Emirates, which contains a small zoo for the Middle East animals?
Sharjah National Park (0.2 sq mi / 0.6 km^2)

2065. What are administrative divisions called in the United Arab Emirates?
Emirates

2066. How many emirates does United Arab Emirates have?
7

2067. What is the largest emirate that accounts for 87 percent of the United Arab Emirates' total area?
Abu Dhabi (15,933 sq mi / 67,340 km^2)

2068. How large is the smallest emirate, Ajman?
100 sq mi / 259 km^2

2069. What is the climate of the United Arab Emirates?
Desert; cooler in eastern mountains

2070. What are the natural resources of the United Arab Emirates?
Petroleum and natural gas

2071. What are the natural hazards of the United Arab Emirates?
Frequent sand and dust storms

2072. What are the religions of the United Arab Emirates?
Muslim 96% (Shia 16%), other (includes Christian, Hindu)

2073. What are the ethnic groups of the United Arab Emirates?
Emirati 19%, other Arab and Iranian 23%, South Asian 50%, other expatriates (includes Westerners and East Asians) 8%

Uzbekistan

2074. What is the official name of Uzbekistan?
Republic of Uzbekistan

2075. Which country borders Uzbekistan to the southwest?
Turkmenistan
2076. Which country borders Uzbekistan to the south?
Afghanistan
2077. Which country borders Uzbekistan to the north and west?
Kazakstan
2078. Which country borders Uzbekistan to the southeast?
Tajikistan
2079. Which country borders Uzbekistan to the east?
Kyrgyzstan
2080. Why is Uzbekistan a doubly landlocked country?
Because it is landlocked by landlocked courtiers
2081. What is the national anthem of Uzbekistan?
National Anthem of the Republic of Uzbekistan
2082. What is the capital of Uzbekistan?
Tashkent (the largest city)
2083. What is the official language of Uzbekistan?
Uzbek
2084. What type of government does Uzbekistan have?
Presidential Republic
2085. When did Russia incorporate all three khanates (all of the present-day Uzbekistan)?
February 19th, 1876
2086. When was the Uzbek Soviet Socialist Republic established?
December 5th, 1924
2087. When did Tajikistan become a separate Soviet socialist republic?
December 5th, 1929
2088. When did Uzbekistan gain independence from Soviet Union?
September 1st, 1991
2089. What is the area of Uzbekistan?
172,696 sq mi / 447,400 km^2
2090. How long is the coastline of Uzbekistan?
0 mi / 0 km (landlocked)
2091. What is the population of Uzbekistan?
28,661,637 (by 2013)
2092. What is the currency of Uzbekistan?
Uzbekistan Som
2093. What is the geographical feature of the terrain of Uzbekistan?
Mostly flat-to-rolling sandy desert with dunes; broad, flat intensely irrigated river valleys along course of the Amu Darya, Syr Darya (Sirdaryo), and Zarafshon; Fergana Valley in east surrounded by mountainous Tajikistan and Kyrgyzstan; shrinking Aral Sea in west
2094. What is the longest river in Uzbekistan, located in Afghanistan, Tajikistan, Turkmenistan, and Uzbekistan?
Amu Darya (1,600 mi / 2,574 km)
2095. The Zarafshon River (also called Zeravshan), located in Tajikistan and Uzbekistan, is a tributary of which river?

Amu Darya
2096. What is the largest lake in Uzbekistan, located in Kazakhstan and Uzbekistan?
Aral Sea
2097. What is the largest lake entirely in Uzbekistan?
Aydar Lake (about 1,200 sq mi / 3,000 km^2)
2098. What is the highest point of Uzbekistan?
Adelunga Toghi (14,111 ft / 4,301 m)
2099. Adelunga Toghi is located in which mountain range?
Pskem Mountains
2100. What is the lowest point of Uzbekistan?
Sariqarnish Kuli (-39 ft / -12 m)
2101. What are leading cities of the Silk Road that are located in Uzbekistan?
Samarkand, Bukhara, and Khiva
2102. What are national parks in Uzbekistan?
Chatkal National Park and Zaamin National Park
2103. How large is Chatkal National Park, located in northeastern Uzbekistan, which is famous for mountain steppes, mountain forests, alpine meadows, river valleys and floodplain forests?
220 sq mi / 570 km^2
2104. How large is Zaamin National Park, located in the central Uzbekistan, which has dramatic intersections of river, mountain, and desert ecosystems?
60 sq mi / 156 km^2
2105. What are administrative divisions called in Uzbekistan?
Provinces
2106. How many provinces does Uzbekistan have?
12 (plus 1 autonomous republic and 1 city)
2107. What is the climate of Uzbekistan?
Mostly midlatitude desert, long, hot summers, mild winters; semiarid grassland in east
2108. What are the natural resources of Uzbekistan?
Adelunga Toghi
2109. What are the religions of Uzbekistan?
Muslim 88% (mostly Sunnis), Eastern Orthodox 9%, other 3%
2110. What are the ethnic groups of Uzbekistan?
Uzbek 80%, Russian 5.5%, Tajik 5%, Kazakh 3%, Karakalpak 2.5%, Tatar 1.5%, other 2.5%

Vietnam

2111. What is the official name of Vietnam?
Socialist Republic of Vietnam
2112. Which country borders Vietnam to the north?
China
2113. Which countries border Vietnam to the west?
Laos and Cambodia
2114. Which body of water lies to the south and east of Vietnam?
South China Sea

2115. Which body of water lies to the east Vietnam?
Gulf of Tonkin

2116. Which body of water lies to the west of Vietnam?
Gulf of Thailand

2117. What is the motto of Vietnam?
Independence - Freedom - Happiness

2118. What is the national anthem of Vietnam?
Sound of Singing Soldiers

2119. What is the capital of Vietnam?
Hanoi

2120. What is the largest city of Vietnam?

Ho Chi Minh City

2121. What is the official language of Vietnam?
Vietnamese

2122. What type of government does Vietnam have?
Socialist republic, Single Party communist State

2123. Vietnam a tributary state of which country for much of its history before 19th century?
China

2124. Which country began the conquest of Vietnam in 1858 and completed by 1884?
France

2125. When was the French Indochina established, including the present-day Vietnam and Cambodia?
October 17th, 1887

2126. What were capitals of the French Indochina?
Saigon (1887–1901) and Hanoi (1902–1954)

2127. When was Laos added to French Indochina?
October 3rd, 1893

2128. When did North Vietnam gain independence from the French Indochina?
September 2nd, 1945

2129. What was the official name of North Vietnam?
Democratic Republic of Vietnam

2130. What was the capital of North Vietnam?
Hanoi

2131. What type of government did North Vietnam have?
Socialist State

2132. What was the size of North Vietnam?
60,958 sq mi / 157,880 km^2

2133. When did South Vietnam gain independence from the French Indochina?
June 14th, 1949

2134. What was the official name of South Vietnam?
Republic of Vietnam

2135. What was the capital of South Vietnam?
Saigon

2136. What type of government did South Vietnam have?
Republic

2137. What was the size of South Vietnam?
67,108 sq mi / 173,809 km^2

2138. What was the First Indochina War (also called French Indochina War, Anti-French War, Franco-Vietnamese War, Franco-Vietminh War, Indochina War, Dirty War, or Anti-French Resistance War) during December 19, 1946 – August 1, 1954?
It was a war fought in the French Indochina between French supported South Vietnam and North Vietnam; a North Vietnam victory; Departure of the French from Indochina

2139. What were the contents of Geneva Accords of 1954?
Vietnam was divided into the Communist North and anti-Communist South

2140. What was the South Vietnamese coup in November 1963?
It was a successful CIA-backed coup led by General Duong Van Minh to assassinate then

president of South Vietnam, Ngo Dinh Diem

2141. What was the Vietnam War (also called Second Indochina War, American War) during November 1st, 1955 – April 30st, 1975?
It was a Cold War military conflict that occurred in Vietnam, Laos, and Cambodia, which was between North Vietnam, supported by China, Soviet Union and other communist nations, and South Vietnam, supported by the United States and other anti-communist nations

2142. On April 30th, 1975, which event marked the end of Vietnam War?
Fall of Saigon (Saigon was captured by North Vietnam)

2143. Saigon was renamed to what?
Ho Chi Minh City

2144. When were North and South Vietnam unified under North Vietnamese rule as the Socialist Republic of Vietnam?
July 2nd, 1976

2145. What was the Cambodian-Vietnamese War during May 1975 – December 1989?
Vietnam invaded Cambodia and deposed the Khmer Rouge regime

2146. What was the Sino-Vietnamese War (also called Third Indochina War) during February 17th, 1979 – March 16th, 1979?
The Chinese invaded Vietnam as "punishment" for the Vietnamese invasion of Cambodia, and withdrew a month later to prewar positions

2147. What is the area of Vietnam?
127,847 sq mi / 331,210 km^2

2148. How long is Vietnam, extending north to south?
1,025 mi / 1,650 km

2149. How wide is Vietnam at its narrowest point?
31 mi / 50 km

2150. How long is the coastline of Vietnam?
2,140 mi / 3,444 km (excludes islands)

2151. What is the population of Vietnam?
92,477,857 (by 2013)

2152. What is the currency of Vietnam?
Dong

2153. What is the geographical feature of the terrain of Vietnam?
Low, flat delta in south and north; central highlands; hilly, mountainous in far north and northwest

2154. What is the highest point of Vietnam?
Fan Si Pan (10,315 ft / 3,144 m)

2155. Why is Fan Si Pan called the Roof of Indochina?
Because it is the highest mountain in Indochina

2156. What is the lowest point of Vietnam?
South China Sea (0 ft / 0 m)

2157. Which waterfall is on the Quy Xuan River, straddling the Sino-Vietnamese border?
Detian - Banyue Falls

2158. What is the Mekong Delta?
A region in southwestern Vietnam where the Mekong River approaches and empties into

the sea through a network of distributaries

2159. What is the Red River Delta?
A flat, triangular region in northeastern Vietnam where the Red River flows into Gulf of Tonkin

2160. What is the highest point of Annamite Range, located in Vietnam, Laos, and Cambodia?
Ngoc Pan (8,524 ft / 2,598 m)

2161. What is the longest river in Vietnam, located in China, Burma, Laos, Thailand, Cambodia, and Vietnam?
Mekong River (2,600 mi / 4,184 km)

2162. Which river has the longest shoreline 292 mi / (470 km) within Vietnam?
Red River

2163. Which national parks are located in Vietnam?
Ba Be National Park, Ba Vi National Park, Bach Ma National Park, Bai Tu Long National Park, Ben En National Park, Bidoup Nui Ba National Park, Bu Gia Map National Park, Cape Ca Mau National Park, Cat Ba Island, Cat Ba National Park, Cat Tien National Park, Chu Mom Ray National Park, Chu Yang Sin National Park, Con Dao National Park, Cuc Phuong National Park, Hoang Lien National Park, Kon Ka Kinh National Park, Lo Go Xa Mat National Park, Lower U Minh National Park, Nui Chua National Park, Phong Nha-Ke Bang National Park, Phu Quoc National Park, Phuoc Binh National Park, Pu Mat National Park, Tam Dao National Park, Tram Chim National Park, U Minh Thuong National Park, Vu Quang Vu Quang National Park, Xuan Son National Park, Xuan Thuy National Park, and Yok Don National Park

2164. What is the largest national park, located in the southern Vietnam, which is famous for the mosaic of deciduous forest and semi-evergreen (mixed deciduous) forest?
Yok Don National Park (446 sq mi / 1,155 km^2)

2165. What is the second largest national park, located in the central Vietnam, which has 2,461 plant species?
Pu Mat National Park (352 sq mi / 911 km²)

2166. What is the third largest national park, located in the central Vietnam, which protects the large karst region with 300 caves and grottoes?
Phong Nha-Ke Bang National Park (331 sq mi / 857 km²)

2167. What is the largest lake in Vietnam, located in Ba Be National Park?
Ba Be Lake (2.5 sq mi / 6.5 km²)

2168. What are administrative divisions called in Vietnam?
Provinces

2169. How many provinces does Vietnam have?
58 (plus 5 municipalities)

2170. What is the climate of Vietnam?
Tropical in south; monsoonal in north with hot, rainy season (May to September) and warm, dry season (October to March)

2171. What are the natural resources of Vietnam?
Phosphates, coal, manganese, bauxite, chromate, offshore oil and gas deposits, timber, and hydropower

2172. What are the natural hazards of Vietnam?
Occasional typhoons (May to January) with extensive flooding, especially in the Mekong River delta

2173. What are the religions of Vietnam?

Buddhist 9.3%, Catholic 6.7%, Hoa Hao 1.5%, Cao Dai 1.1%, Protestant 0.5%, Muslim 0.1%, none 80.8%

2174. What are the ethnic groups of Vietnam?

Kinh (Viet) 86.2%, Tay 1.9%, Thai 1.7%, Muong 1.5%, Khome 1.4%, Hoa 1.1%, Nun 1.1%, Hmong 1%, others 4.1%

West Bank (Disputed)

2175. What is West Bank's status?

Israeli-occupied and the status is subject to the Israeli-Palestinian Interim Agreement

2176. Which country borders West Bank to the east?

Jordan

2177. Which country borders West Bank to the south, west and north?

Israel
2178. What is the largest city of West Bank?
East Jerusalem
2179. What is the official language of West Bank?
Arabic
2180. Who is in charge of the de facto government in West Bank?
Abbas (Palestinian Authority President)
2181. What is the area of West Bank?
2,262 sq mi / 5,860 km^2
2182. How long is the coastline of West Bank?
0 mi / 0 km (landlocked)
2183. What is the population of West Bank?
2,676,740 (by 2013)
2184. What are currencies of West Bank?
New Israeli Shekel and Jordanian Dinar
2185. What is the geographical feature of the terrain of West Bank?
Mostly rugged dissected upland, some vegetation in west, but barren in east
2186. What is the highest point of West Bank?
Tall Asur (3,353 ft / 1,022 m)
2187. What is the lowest point of West Bank?
Dead Sea (-1,339 ft / -408 m)
2188. What is the climate of West Bank?
Temperate; temperature and precipitation vary with altitude, warm to hot summers, cool to mild winters
2189. What are the natural resources of West Bank?
Arable land
2190. What are the natural hazards of West Bank?
Droughts
2191. What are the religions of West Bank?
Muslim 75% (predominantly Sunni), Jewish 17%, Christian and other 8%
2192. What are the ethnic groups of West Bank?
Palestinian Arab and other 83%, Jewish 17%

Yemen

2193. What is the official name of Yemen?
Republic of Yemen
2194. Which country borders Yemen to the north?
Saudi Arabia
2195. Which country borders Yemen to the east?
Oman
2196. Which body of water lies to the west of Yemen?
Red Sea
2197. Which bodies of water lie to the south of Yemen?
Arabian Sea and Gulf of Aden

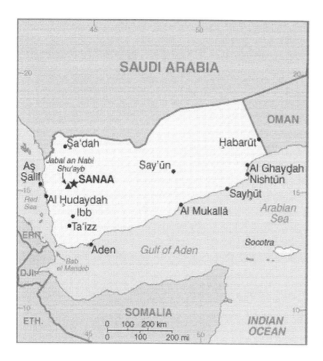

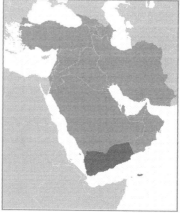

2198. What is the largest island in Yemen, where a third of its plant life can only be found on the island?

Socotra

2199. What is the motto of Yemen?

God, Nation, Revolution, Unity

2200. What is the national anthem of Yemen?

United Republic

2201. What is the capital of Yemen?

Sanaa (the largest city)

2202. What is the official language of Yemen?

Arabic

2203. What type of government does Yemen have?

Republic

2204. When did South Yemen become part of Ottoman Empire?

July 27th, 1538

2205. When did South Yemen become a British protectorate?

September 1839

2206. When did South Yemen gain independence from the United Kingdom?

November 30th, 1967

2207. What was the capital of South Yemen?

Aden

2208. In which year did North Yemen become part of the Ottoman Empire?

1876

2209. When did North Yemen gain independence from the Ottoman Empire?

October 30th, 1918

2210. What was the capital of North Yemen?

Sanaa

2211. When were South Yemen and North Yemen unified?

May 22nd, 1990

2212. What is the area of Yemen?

203,796 sq mi / 527,968 km^2

2213. How long is the coastline of Yemen?

1,184 mi / 1,906 km

2214. What is the population of Yemen?

25,408,288 (by 2013)

2215. What is the currency of Yemen?

Yemeni Rial

2216. What is the geographical feature of the terrain of Yemen?

Mostly desert; hot and humid along west coast; temperate in western mountains affected by seasonal monsoon; extraordinarily hot, dry, harsh desert in east

2217. What is the highest point of Yemen?

Jabal an Nabi Shu'ayb (12,031 ft / 3,667 m)

2218. What is the lowest point of Yemen?

Arabian Sea (0 ft / 0 m)

2219. What are administrative divisions called in Yemen?

Governorates

2220. How many governorates does Yemen have?

21

2221. What is the climate of Yemen?

Mostly desert; hot and humid along west coast; temperate in western mountains affected by seasonal monsoon; extraordinarily hot, dry, harsh desert in east

2222. What are the natural resources of Yemen?

Petroleum, fish, rock salt, marble; small deposits of coal, gold, lead, nickel, and copper; fertile soil in west

2223. What are the natural hazards of Yemen?

Sandstorms and dust storms in summer

2224. What are the religions of Yemen?

Muslim including Shaf'i (Sunni) and Zaydi (Shia), small numbers of Jewish, Christian, and Hindu

2225. What are the ethnic groups of Yemen?

Predominantly Arab; but also Afro-Arab, South Asians, Europeans

Miscellaneous

2226. Himalayas are located in which countries?
Bhutan, China, India, Nepal, Pakistan, Burma, and Afghanistan

2227. How many mountains are there in Himalayas over 23,622 ft (7,200 m)?
More than 100

2228. What is the highest mountain in the world, located in Nepal and China?
Mount Everest (29,035 ft / 8,850 m)

2229. Mount Everest is located in which mountain range?
Mahalangur Himal, a subrange of the Himalayas

2230. What is the second highest mountain in the world, located in Pakistan, India and China?
K2 (28,251 ft / 8,611 m)

2231. K2 is located in which mountain range?
Baltoro Muztagh, a subrange of Karakoram

2232. What is the third highest mountain in the world, located in India and Nepal?
Kangchenjunga (28,169 ft / 8,586 m)

2233. Kangchenjunga is located in which mountain range?
Himalayas

2234. What is the fourth highest mountain in the world, located in Nepal and China?
Lhotse (27,940 ft / 8,516 m)

2235. Lhotse is located in which mountain range?
Mahalangur Himal

2236. What is the fifth highest mountain in the world, located in Nepal and China?
Makalu (27,766 ft / 8,463 m)

2237. Makalu is located in which mountain range?
Mahalangur Himal

2238. What is the sixth highest mountain in the world, located in Nepal and China?
Cho Oyu (26,906 ft / 8,201 m)

2239. Cho Oyu is located in which mountain range?
Mahalangur Himal

2240. What is the seventh highest mountain in the world, located in Nepal?
Dhaulagiri (26,795 ft / 8,167 m)

2241. Dhaulagiri is located in which mountain range?
Dhaulagiri Himal, a subrange of the Himalayas

2242. What is the eighth highest mountain in the world, located in Nepal?
Manaslu (26,759 ft / 8,156 m)

2243. Manaslu is located in which mountain range?
Mansiri Himal, a subrange of the Himalayas

2244. What is the tenth highest mountain in the world, located in Nepal?
Annapurna (26,545 ft / 8,091 m)

2245. Annapurna is located in which mountain range?
Himalayas

2246. Which rivers rise in the Himalayas?
Ganges, Indus, Brahmaputra, Yangtze, Mekong, Salween, Red River, Xunjiang, Chao Phraya,

Irrawaddy River, Amu Darya, Syr Darya, Tarim River and Yellow River

2247. How long is the Ganges River, which flows from India to Bangladesh?
1,560 mi / 2,510 km

2248. What is the source of the Ganges River?
Gangotri Glacier (India)

2249. What is the mouth of the Ganges River?
Ganges Delta (Bangladesh)

2250. How long is the Indus River, which flows from China to India and Pakistan?
1,976 mi / 3,180 km

2251. What is the source of the Indus River?
Confluence of the Sengge River and Gar River (China)

2252. What is the mouth of the Indus River?
Sapta Sindhu (Pakistan)

2253. How long is the Brahmaputra River, starting as the Yarlung Tsangpo River in China, passing through India as the Dihang River, to Bangladesh as the Jamuna River?
1,800 mi /2,900 km

2254. What is the source of the Brahmaputra River?
South Tibet Valley (China)

2255. What is the mouth of the Brahmaputra River?
Ganges Delta (Bangladesh)

2256. How long is the Yangtze River in China?
3,915 mi / 6,300 km

2257. What is the source of the Yangtze River?
A glacier on the Geladandong Mountain

2258. What is the mouth of the Yangtze River?
East China Sea

2259. How long is the Mekong River, which flows through China, Burma, Laos, Thailand, Cambodia, and Vietnam?
2,600 mi / 4,184 km

2260. What is the source of the Mekong River?
Lasagongma Spring (China)

2261. What is the mouth of the Mekong River?
Mekong Delta (Vietnam)

2262. How long is the Salween River, from China, passing Burma, to Thailand?
1,749 mi / 2,815

2263. What is the source of the Salween River?
Qinghai Mountains (China)

2264. What is the mouth of the Salween River?
Andaman Sea (Thailand)

2265. How long is the Red River, from China to Vietnam?
730 mi / 1,175 km

2266. What is the source of the Red River?
Mountains in Dali (China)

2267. What is the mouth of the Red River?
Gulf of Tonkin (Vietnam)

2268. How long is the Xunjiang River in China?
124 mi / 199 km
2269. How long is the Chao Phraya River in Thailand?
231 mi / 372 km
2270. What is the source of the Chao Phraya River?
Confluence of the Ping River and the Nan River
2271. What is the mouth of the Chao Phraya River?
Gulf of Thailand
2272. How long is the Irrawaddy River in Burma?
1,348 mi / 2,170 km
2273. What is the source of the Irrawaddy River?
Mali River
2274. What is the mouth of the Irrawaddy River?
Andaman Sea
2275. How long is the Amu Darya, located in Afghanistan, Tajikistan, Turkmenistan, and Uzbekistan?
1,600 mi / 2,574 km
2276. What is the source of the Amu Darya?
Pamir River (Afghanistan)
2277. What is the mouth of the Amu Darya?
Aral Sea (Uzbekistan)
2278. How long is the Syr Darya, located in Kazakhstan, Kyrgyzstan, Uzbekistan and Tajikistan?
1,374 mi / 2,212 km
2279. What is the source of the Syr Darya?
Naryn River and Kara Darya River
2280. What is the mouth of the Syr Darya?
Aral Sea (Tajikistan)
2281. How long is the Tarim River in China?
1,261 mi / 2,030 km
2282. What are sources of the Tarim River?
Aksu River, Yarkand River, Khotan River, and Kashgar River
2283. What is the mouth of the Tarim River?
Taitema Lake
2284. How long is the Yellow River in China?
3,395 mi / 5,464 km
2285. What is the source of the Yellow River?
Bayan Har Mountains
2286. What is the mouth of the Yellow River?
Bohai Sea
2287. What is the longest river in Asia, and the third longest in the world?
Yangtze River
2288. What is the second longest River in Asia, and the fifth longest in the world?
Yenisey River (3,534 mi / 5,526 km)
2289. What is the source of the Yenisey River, located in Mongolia and Russia?
Khangai Mountains (Mongolia)

2290. What is the mouth of the Yenisey River?
Kara Sea (Russia)
2291. What is the third longest River in Asia, and the sixth longest in the world?
Yellow River
2292. What is the fourth longest River in Asia, and the seventh longest in the world?
The Ob-Irtysh River (3,354 mi / 5,398 km)
2293. What is the source of the Ob-Irtysh River in Russia?
Altai Mountains
2294. What is the mouth of the Ob-Irtysh River?
Gulf of Ob
2295. What is the fifth longest River in Asia, and the ninth longest in the world?
Amur Darya (also called Heilong) (2,744 mi / 4,416 km)
2296. What are sources of the Amur Darya, located in Mongolia, Russia, and China?
Onon River-Shilka River (Mongolia), Kherlen River-Argun River (Mongolia)
2297. What is the mouth of the Amur Darya?
Tatar Strait (Russia)
2298. What is the sixth longest River in Asia, and the tenth longest in the world?
Lena River (2,734 mi / 4,400 km)
2299. What is the source of the Lena River in Russia?
Baikal Mountains
2300. What is the mouth of the Lena River in Russia?
Laptev Sea
2301. What is the seventh longest River in Asia, and the twelfth longest in the world?
Mekong River
2302. What is the eighth longest River in Asia?
Shatt Al Arab-Euphrates River (2,236 mi / 3,598 km)
2303. What is the source of the Shatt Al Arab-Euphrates River, located in Iraq, Turkey, Iran, and Syria?
Tigris River and Euphrates River
2304. What is the mouth of the Shatt Al Arab-Euphrates River?
Persian Gulf
2305. What is the ninth longest River in Asia?
Indus River
2306. What is the tenth longest River in Asia?
Syr Darya
2307. How long is the Tigris River, located in Turkey, Syria, and Iraq?
1,150 mi / 1,850 km
2308. What is the source of the Tigris River?
Lake Hazar (Turkey)
2309. What is the mouth of the Tigris River?
Shatt al-Arab (Iraq)
2310. What is Pamir Mountains?
A mountain range in Central Asia formed by the junction of Himalayas, Tian Shan, Karakoram, Kunlun, and Hindu Kush ranges
2311. What is the nickname of the Pamir Mountains?

Roof of the World

2312. Pamir Mountains spread to which courtiers?
Tajikistan, Kyrgyzstan, Afghanistan, Pakistan, and China

2313. What is the highest point of Pamir Mountains, located in Tajikistan?
Ismail Samani Peak (24,590 ft / 7,495 m)

2314. Tien Shan is a mountain range located in which countries?
China, Pakistan, India, Kazakhstan, Kyrgyzstan, and Uzbekistan

2315. What is the highest point of Tien Shan?
Jengish Chokosu (also called Pobeda Peak, 24,406 ft / 7,439 m)

2316. What is world's fifth largest desert by size, located in Mongolia and China?
Gobi Desert (500,002 sq mi / 1,295,000 km^2)

2317. Gobi Desert is located in which plateau, located in Mongolia and China?
Mongolian Plateau

2318. Ariana was a region of the eastern countries of ancient Persia, next to the Indian subcontinent. Which present-day countries are included in Ariana?
Afghanistan, most of Tajikistan, eastern Iran, southern Turkmenistan, southern Uzbekistan and western Pakistan

2319. Arachosia was a region of the Iranian land of Harauti. Which present-day countries are included in Arachosia?
Southeastern Afghanistan and southwestern Pakistan

2320. Khorasan was a historical geographic region. Which present-day countries are included in Khorasan?
Northeastern Iran, northwestern Afghanistan, and southern parts of Turkmenistan and Uzbekistan

2321. What was the Paratethys Sea?
An ancient large shallow sea that stretched from the region north of the Alps over Central Europe to Aral Sea in western Asia

2322. What are the present-day remnants of the Paratethys Sea?
Black Sea (Europe), Caspian Sea, and Aral Sea

2323. What is the largest enclosed body of water in the world?
Caspian Sea (143,200 sq mi / 371,000 km^2)

2324. Caspian Sea is bordered by which countries?
Iran, Russia, Kazakhstan, Turkmenistan, and Azerbaijan

2325. Caspian Sea is divided into which three physical regions?
Northern Caspian, Middle Caspian, and Southern Caspian

2326. Northern Caspian accounts for what percentage of the total water volume?
1 %

2327. Middle Caspian accounts for what percentage of the total water volume?
33%

2328. Southern Caspian accounts for what percentage of the total water volume?
66%

2329. What is the largest island among more than 26 islands in Caspian Sea?
Ogurja Ada

2330. What is the longest river among 130 inflows to Caspian Sea?
Volga River (Europe, 2,294 mi / 3,692 km)

2331. What is the second longest inflow to Caspian Sea, which forms part of the boundary between Europe and Asia?
Ural River (1,509 mi / 2,428 km)

2332. What is the third longest inflow to Caspian Sea, located in Turkey, Georgia, and Azerbaijan?
Kura River (also called Kur, Mt'k'vari, 941 mi / 1,515 km)

2333. What tributaries does Kura River have?
Lori River, Alazani River, Khrami River, and Aras River

2334. How long is Lori River, located in Georgia and Azerbaijan?
199 mi / 320 km

2335. How long is Khrami River, located in Georgia and Azerbaijan?
125 mi / 201 km

2336. How long is Alazani River, located in Georgia and Azerbaijan?
218 mi / 351 km

2337. How long is Aras River, located in Turkey, Armenia, Iran, and Azerbaijan?
665 mi / 1,072 km

2338. What was the result of the Pacific War (also called Asia-Pacific War), as a part of World War II that took place in the Pacific Ocean, its islands, and in the Far East during December 7th, 1941–September 2nd, 1945?
Allied victory

2339. What was the South-East Asian theatre of World War II?
It was the name given to the campaigns of the Pacific War in Burma, British India, Thailand, French Indochina, British Malaya, Singapore, and British Ceylon

2340. What is the Asian Century?
A term used to describe the belief that, if certain demographic and economic trends persist, the twenty-first century will be dominated by Asian politics and culture

2341. What is the Four Asian Tigers?
The term refers to highly developed economies of Hong Kong, Singapore, South Korea and Taiwan between the early 1960s and 1990s

2342. What is the Tiger Cub Economies?
The term refers to the economies of four dominant countries in the Southeast Asia, following Four Asian Tigers. The four countries are Indonesia, Malaysia, Philippines, and Thailand

2343. Levant describes the Eastern Mediterranean at large, but can be used as a geographical term that denotes a large area in Western Asia. What countries are included in Levant?
Lebanon, Syria, Jordan, and Iraq (occasionally Cyprus, Sinai, and Israel)

2344. Caucasus is a geopolitical region at the border of Europe and Asia. It is home to which mountain range?
Caucasus Mountains (Greater Caucasus, Lesser Caucasus)

2345. While North Caucasus comprises republics in Russia, South Caucasus comprises which counties?
Armenia, Azerbaijan, and Georgia

2346. What is Palestine?
It is a conventional name that is used to describe a geographic region between the Mediterranean Sea and the Jordan River, and various adjoining lands. As a geographic term, Palestine can refer to "ancient Palestine," an area that includes the present-day Israel, the

Israeli-occupied Palestinian territories, part of Jordan, Lebanon, and Syria

2347. What are Israeli-occupied Palestinian territories?
Gaza Strip and West Bank

2348. When did the United Kingdom occupy Palestine?
September 26th, 1918

2349. Palestine became the Palestine League of Nations mandate under which country on July 24th, 1922?
United Kingdom

2350. What was the United Nations Partition Plan for Palestine on November 29th, 1947?
It recommended the termination of the British Mandate for Palestine and the partition of the territory into two states, one Jewish and one Arab, with the Jerusalem-Bethlehem area being under special international protection, administered by the United Nations

2351. United Nations Partition Plan for Palestine was rejected by leaders of which side, Israel or Arab?
Arab

2352. The day after the United Nations Partition Plan for Palestine (November 30th, 1947), what war started?
1947–1948 Civil War in Mandatory Palestine, the clash between Jewish and Arab communities of Palestine

2353. The United Kingdom announced to unilaterally withdraw from the Palestine mandate of Palestine by when?
May 15th, 1948

2354. When did the Jewish community in Palestine publish the Declaration of Independence as the State of Israel?
May 14th, 1948

2355. Which five Arab armies crossed into the former Mandate on May 14th, 1948?
Egypt, Iraq, Jordan, Lebanon and Syria

2356. When did All-Palestine Government declare Palestine independent with capital at Jerusalem?
October 1st, 1948

2357. Which set of agreements, signed during 1949 between Israel and neighboring Egypt, Lebanon, Jordan, and Syria, ended Arab-Israeli War?
1949 Armistice Agreements

2358. What was the result of 1948 Arab-Israeli War?
State of Israel established from captured territories, Jordanian occupation of West Bank, and Egyptian occupation of Gaza Strip

2359. What was called for 1947 – 1948 Civil War in Mandatory Palestine and 1948 Arab–Israeli War?
1948 Palestine war

2360. What was the Suez Crisis (also called Tripartite Aggression) during October 29th, 1956 – March 1957?
A military attack on Egypt by Britain, France, and Israel caused by the nationalization of the Suez Canal

2361. What was the Six-Day War (also called 1967 Arab-Israeli War, the Third Arab-Israeli War, Six Days' War, an-Naksah, or the June War) during June 5th, 1967 – June 10th, 1967?

A war between Israeli and the armies of the neighboring states of 9 Arab counties (Egypt, Jordan, Syria, Iraq, Saudi Arabia, Sudan, Tunisia, Morocco and Algeria)

2362. What was the result of Six-Day War?

Israel had gained control of Sinai Peninsula, Gaza Strip, West Bank, East Jerusalem, and Golan Heights

2363. Why was 1973 Arab-Israeli War (also called Ramadan War, October War, Fourth Arab-Israeli War), during October 6th, 1973 – October 26th, 1973, called the Yom Kippur War?

Because October 6th, 1973 was the Jewish holy day Yom Kippur

2364. What happened during the Yom Kippur War?

Egyptian forces struck eastward across the Suez Canal and pushed the Israelis back, while the Syrians advanced from the north. Iraqi forces joined the war and, in addition, Syria received some support from Jordan, Libya, and the smaller Arab states. The attacks caught Israel off guard, and Israel then forced the Syrians and Egyptians back

2365. When was the Palestine Liberation Organization (PLO) granted permanent observer status in the United Nations?

November 10th, 1975

2366. The Camp David Accords were signed by leaders of which two countries on September 17th, 1978 at the White House?

Egypt and Israel

2367. Which treaty was signed in Washington, DC on March 26th, 1979, following the 1978 Camp David Accords?

1979 Egypt–Israel Peace Treaty: the mutual recognition of each country by the other, the cessation of war that had existed since 1948 Arab-Israeli War, and the complete withdrawal by Israel from the rest of the Sinai Peninsula which Israel had captured during the Six-Day War in 1967

2368. When did Jordan abandon its claim for the West Bank in favor of a peaceful resolution between Israel and PLO?

July 31st, 1988

2369. Why was the Oslo Accords (also called Declaration of Principles on Interim Self-Government Arrangements, Declaration of Principles, DOP), signed on September 13th, 1993, a milestone in the ongoing Palestinian-Israeli conflict?

Because it was the first direct, face-to-face agreement between Israel and PLO

2370. What were main features of Oslo Accords?

Oslo Accords provided the creation of the Palestinian Authority (PA), which administrated the territory under its control, and called for the withdrawal of Israel Defense Forces (IDF) from parts of Gaza Strip and West Bank

2371. When was the Palestinian Authority created to administer most of Gaza Strip and parts of West Bank?

May 4th, 1994

2372. What was the Israel-Jordan Treaty of Peace (also called Treaty of Peace between the State of Israel and the Hashemite Kingdom of Jordan, Wadi Araba Treaty) that was signed on October 26, 1994?

It normalized relations between Israel and Jordan, and resolved territorial disputes between them

2373. In which year did Israeli forces occupy the Palestinian Authority areas?

2002

2374. When did Israel withdraw settlements from the Gaza Strip?
September 12th, 2005

2375. Whose forces seized control of the Gaza Strip from June 14th, 2007?
Hamas

2376. What is the lowest lake in the world?
Dead Sea (-1,339 ft / -408 m)

2377. What is Dead Sea's saltiness?
33.7% salinity

2378. Which countries/territories border Dead Sea?
Jordan (east), Israel (west), and West Bank (west)

2379. What is the inflow of Dead Sea?
Jordan River (the longest salt river in the world, 156 mi / 251 km)

2380. How large is Dead Sea?
310 sq mi / 810 km^2

2381. What is Canaan?
An ancient term for a region at present-day Israel, Lebanon, Palestinian territories and adjoining coastal lands, including parts of Jordan, Syria and northeastern Egypt

2382. What were contents of the Sykes-Picot Agreement, concluded on May 16th, 1916?
It was a secret agreement between the United Kingdom, France, and Russia; the United Kingdom was allocated the present-day Jordan, southern Iraq, and a small area around Haifa (Israel); France was allocated southeastern Turkey, northern Iraq, Syria and Lebanon; Russia was allocated Constantinople, Turkish Straits and Ottoman Armenian vilayets

2383. What is Kashmir?
It is a disputed area in the northwestern region of Indian subcontinent. It includes Indian administered state of Jammu and Kashmir (Jammu, Kashmir, and Ladakh), Pakistani administered Gilgit-Baltistan and Azad Kashmir, and Chinese-administered regions of Aksai Chin and Trans-Karakoram Tract

2384. What was Kashmir and Jammu?
A princely state in the British Raj during 1846 – 1947

2385. What was the Indo-Pakistani War of 1947 (also called First Kashmir War) during October 21st, 1947 – December 31st, 1948?
A military conflict between India and Pakistan; Kashmir and Jammu dissolved to become Indian administered state of Jammu and Kashmir (Jammu, Kashmir, and Ladakh), Pakistani administered Gilgit-Baltistan and Azad Kashmir

2386. What was the Sino-Indian War (also called Sino-Indian Border Conflict) during October 20th, 1962 – November 21st, 1962?
A military conflict between China and India for the disputed Himalayan border; China controlled Tibet (excluding Tawang and area south of McMahon Line) and retained Aksai Chin area while India controlled North-East Frontier (South Tibet, Arunachal) area

2387. What was the Indo-Pakistani War of 1965 (also called Second Kashmir War) during August, 1965 – September 23rd, 1965?
A military conflict between India and Pakistan; no permanent territorial changes

2388. What was the Indo-Pakistani War of 1971 (also called Third Kashmir War) during December 3rd, 1971 – December 16th, 1971?

A military conflict between India and Pakistan; a decisive Indian victory, which led the secession of East Pakistan from Pakistan as the independent state of Bangladesh

2389. What is the Indo-Gangetic Plain (also called Northern Plains, North Indian River Plain)?
A large and fertile plain encompassing most of northern and eastern India, the most populous parts of Pakistan, parts of southern Nepal and virtually all of Bangladesh; the plain is named after Indus River and Ganges River, the twin river systems that drain it

2390. About how large is the Indo-Gangetic Plain, which is home to nearly 1 billion people (or around 1/7 of the world's population)?
270,000 sq mi / 700,000 km²

2391. What is the Punjab region?
It is a cultural region straddling the border between India and Pakistan, and the region is composed by the Indian state of Punjab and the Pakistani province of Punjab

2392. What is the "five waters" of Punjab region?
Jhelum River, Chenab River, Ravi River, Sutlej River, and Beas River

2393. The "five waters" of Punjab region are tributaries of which river?
Indus River

2394. Which river is the largest in Punjab region?
Jhelum River

2395. In 1932, French Indochina annexed which archipelago and set up a weather station on its Pattle Island?
Paracel Islands

2396. After French, Paracel Islands was maintained by whom?
Vietnam

2397. Paracel Islands was occupied by whom since 1974?
China

2398. What are valuable natural resources surrounding Paracel Islands?
Productive fishing grounds and potential oil and gas reserves

2399. What are valuable natural resources surrounding Spratly Islands?
Productive fishing grounds and potentially oil and gas reserves

2400. Who claims the entire Spratly Islands?
China, Taiwan, and Vietnam

2401. Who claims a portion of the Spratly Islands?
Malaysia and the Philippines

2402. How many islands are occupied by small numbers of military forces from China, Malaysia, the Philippines, Taiwan, and Vietnam?
45

2403. Which country has established a fishing zone that overlaps a southern reef but has not made any formal claim?
Brunei

2404. Which desert is located between the Amu Darya and Syr Darya, and is divided between Kazakhstan, Uzbekistan and (partly) Turkmenistan?
Kyzyl Kum (115,058 sq mi / 298,000 km²)

2405. When did Japan annex Korea?
August 22nd, 1910

2406. When did Korea gain independence from Japan?

August 15th, 1945

2407. Following World War II, Korea was split into which two countries?
North Korea and South Korea

2408. North Korea was occupied by which country during August 26th, 1945 – September 9th, 1948?
Soviet Union

2409. South Korea was occupied by which country during August 26th, 1945 – August 15th, 1948?
United States

2410. An armistice was signed on July 27th, 1953, splitting Korean Peninsula along a demilitarized zone at which line?
The 38th parallel

2411. What are the six independent Turkic countries?
Turkey, Azerbaijan, Turkmenistan, Uzbekistan, Kyrgyzstan and Kazakhstan

2412. What are two main illicit opium-producing areas in Asia?
Golden Triangle and Golden Crescent

2413. Which countries are located in the Golden Triangle?
Burma, Vietnam, Laos, and Thailand

2414. Which countries are located in the Golden Crescent?
Afghanistan, Iran, and Pakistan

2415. Which country in the Golden Crescent does not produce opium?
Iran

2416. When did the "Arab Spring" protests start?
December 18th, 2010

2417. Which countries in Asia saw protests as part of the "Arab Spring" that swept through the region?
Syria, Lebanon, Jordan, Saudi Arabia, Iraq, Kuwait, Oman, and Yemen (overthrown)

Bibliography

- Al Mashriq - the Levant - Lebanon and the Middle, http://almashriq.hiof.no/
- Answers.com - Online Dictionary, Encyclopedia and much more, http://www.answers.com/
- Asterism Travels & Tours - Myanmar, http://www.asterism.info/parks/
- Background Notes, http://www.state.gov/r/pa/ei/bgn/
- CIA – The World Factbook, https://www.cia.gov/library/publications/the-world-factbook/
- Geography Page, http://peakbagger.com/
- Geography Summaries Index – Vaughn's Summaries, http://www.vaughns-1-pagers.com/geography/
- Infoplease: Encyclopedia, Almanac, Atlas, Biographies, Dictionary, Thesaurus. Free online reference, research & homework help, http://www.infoplease.com/
- Official global voting platform of New7Wonders, http://www.new7wonders.com/
- Perry-Castañeda Map Collection - UT Library Online, http://lib.utexas.edu/maps/
- True Knowledge, http://www.trueknowledge.com/
- Wikipedia – The Free Encyclopedia, http://en.wikipedia.org/wiki/Main_Page/
- Wildlife National Parks & Wildlife Sanctuaries of the world, http://www.world-wildlife-adventures.com/
- World Atlas of Maps Flags and Geography Facts and Figures, http://www.worldatlas.com/
- World Database on Protected Areas, http://www.wdpa.org/
- World's Longest Rivers, http://rivers.wonderworld.us/
- World StateMen.org, http://www.worldstatesmen.org/
- World Travel, http://travel.mapsofworld.com/

Other Books

- World Geography Questionnaires: Americas – Countries and Territories in the Region (Volume 1), Kenneth Ma and Jennifer Fu, ISBN-10: 1449553222, ISBN-13: 978-1449553227
- World Geography Questionnaires: Africa – Countries and Territories in the Region (Volume 2), Kenneth Ma and Jennifer Fu, ISBN-10: 1451587074, ISBN-13: 978-1451587074
- World Geography Questionnaires: Oceania & Antarctica – Countries and Territories in the Region (Volume 3), Kenneth Ma and Jennifer Fu, ISBN-10: 1453665250, ISBN-13: 978-1453665251
- World Geography Questionnaires: Europe – Countries and Territories in the Region (Volume 5), Kenneth Ma and Jennifer Fu, ISBN-10: 1453833498, ISBN-13: 978-1453833490
- World Geography Terms – Human Geography and Physical Geography (Volume 6), Kenneth Ma and Jennifer Fu, ISBN-10: 1466329068, ISBN-13: 978-1466329065
- World Geography Questionnaires: United States Geography Questionnaires (Volume 7), Kenneth Ma and Jennifer Fu, ISBN-10: 1477408673, ISBN-13: 978-1477408674
- The Missing Mau, Hermione Ma and Jennifer Fu, ISBN-10: 1451587090, ISBN-13: 978-1451587098
- The Crazy College, Hermione Ma and Jennifer Fu, ISBN-10: 1452851174, ISBN-13: 978-1452851174
- The Revolving Resort, Hermione Ma and Jennifer Fu, ISBN-10: 1453815139, ISBN-13: 978-1453815137
- The Gingerbread Museum of Candy, Omelets, Spinach, Ice, and Biscuits, Hermione Ma, , ISBN-10: 1477543252, ISBN-13: 978-1477543252
- ACE Your Java Interview, Jennifer Fu, ISBN-10: 1484104935, ISBN-13: 978-1484104934
- Bubble, Jennifer Fu, ISBN-10: 1461029120, ISBN-13: 978-1461029120

About the Authors

Kenneth Ma is a twelfth grader at Monta Vista High School in Cupertino, California. He was the National Geography School Bee at Eaton Elementary School in Cupertino when he was in fourth grade, and he was the National Geography School Bee at Kennedy Middle School in Cupertino when he was in sixth grade. He was also a member of the Kennedy Middle School National Geography Challenge Championship team in 2007. In 2007, he was honored with the Outstanding Achievement in Geography Award from his middle school. Besides his interest in Geography, Kenneth is also an avid soccer player.

Jennifer Fu is Kenneth's mom and lives in Cupertino, California. She is a software engineer by day and an aspiring writer by night. She has contributed short stories and novellas to a number of on-line publications in Chinese. Writing a geography book is a new endeavor for her.

27672091R00094

Made in the USA
Lexington, KY
18 November 2013